Discovering
Lake Erie
Wineries

A Travel Guide
to Lake Erie's Wine Country

By Kevin M. Atticks

resonant ◉ publishing

resonant publishing
Baltimore, Maryland

Printed in the United States of America by
Data Reproductions Corporation, Auburn Hills, Michigan.
This book is printed on acid-free paper.

Library of Congress Card Number: 99-091383
ISBN: 0-9668716-3-4

First Edition
10 9 8 7 6 5 4 3 2 1

Photos by Kevin M. Atticks
Sketches by Nickitas Thomarios
Maps by Brian Schumacher
Edited by Judith M. Dobler
Assistant Editors: Mary DeManss,
Alicia Dunphy, Kiersten Laag
Design by resonant design

*Those parties involved in this publication take no responsibility
for errors, typos or misprints. Every effort was made to
ensure the accuracy of information included in this book.*

resonant ⊙ publishing

Baltimore, Maryland
www.resonantgroup.com

*This book
is dedicated to
Andrea,
for her support,
dedication,
and love.*

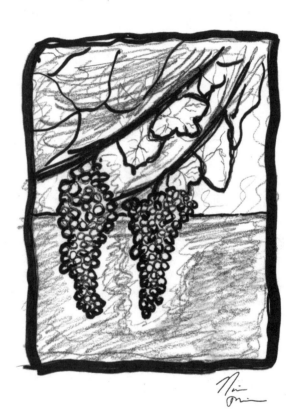

Table of Contents

Introduction...1
Lake Erie Viticultural Regions...4
Quality Alliances...6
Things to Know Before You Go!..8
Map of Lake Erie Wineries..9

Lake Erie's Eastern Region

Introduction...12
Arrowhead Wine Cellars 14
Blueberry Sky Farm Winery 18
Heritage Wine Cellars 22
Johnson Estate Wines...26
Mazza Vineyards 30
Merritt Estate Winery 34
Penn Shore Winery & Vineyards..38
Presque Isle Wine Cellars 42
Schloss Doepkin Winery...46
Vetter Vineyards 50
Woodbury Vineyards..54
Regional Suggestions 58

Lake Erie's Central Region

Introduction...62
Biscotti Family Winery...64
Buccia Vineyard 68
Chalet Debonné Vineyards...72
Claire's Grand River Winery 76
Conneaut Cellars Winery 80
Ferrante Winery & Ristorante...84
Harpersfield Vineyard 88
John Christ Winery 92
Klingshirn Winery..96
Markko Vineyard 100
Old Firehouse Winery 104
Old Mill Winery 108
St. Joseph Vineyard 112
Virant Family Winery 116
Regional Suggestions 120

Lake Erie's Western & U.S. Islands Regions

Introduction 124
Firelands Winery 126
Heineman Winery 130
Johlin Century Winery 134
Kelley's Island Winery 138
Lion Hill Wines 142
Lonz Winery 144
Mon Ami Historic Restaurant & Winery 148
Regional Suggestions 152

Lake Erie's North Region

Introduction 156
Colio Estate Wines 158
D'Angelo Estate Winery 162
LeBlanc Estate Winery 166
Pelee Island Winery 170
Regional Suggestions 174

Good Information

Wine Festivals 178
Wine Associations 179
Wine Publications 180
Where to Buy Lake Erie Wines 181
Useful Wine Terms 182
Other *resonant publishing* titles 184
Notes

Acknowledgements

The following people have provided me with invaluable information during the preparation of this book:

Arnie Esterer, Wes Gerlosky, Andy Horvath,
Bob Mazza, Doug Moorhead, Tara Seib

The following people deserve special recognition, for their friendship and guidance have meant much more than they know:

Ralph, Terry & June Atticks
Brian, Susan & Britni Cartier & Alison Doyle
Andy Ciofalo
Mary DeManss
Judith M. Dobler
Dunph
Elva & Jim Gillespie
Andrea Hirsch
Kathy, Bob & Erik Hirsch
Kiersten Laag
John McGraw
Catherine Mehrling
George P. Miller
John Mohan
Brian Schumacher
Nickitas Thomarios
Paul Thomarios

Thanks to the families and staff of every winery –
your patience and cooperation brought
this project to completion!

Speak softly...
and make a great wine.

— Dave Broom

Introduction

There may be nothing more exciting than discovering a great wine. When driving through Napa Valley, it's almost expected that you will come across wonderful wine. But when that wonderful wine is discovered 40 minutes east of Cleveland, you have something to be thrilled about. That's precisely why I chose to write about Lake Erie's wineries: they are producing gems that are unheard of beyond the immediate region.

I've always loved discovering new wineries. Of course they're not new to everyone, but they're also not known by everyone. Personally, the biggest thrill is finding a spectacular wine that *none of my friends* know about.

In writing my first book, *Discovering Maryland Wineries*, I found more than a few wines that would impress anyone, anywhere in the world. They have become my "house" wines. When I am invited to people's homes for dinners or parties, I bring my newly discovered wines as a gift to my hosts.

Soon after, I get letters and calls asking me where they can find the wine. "Sorry," I say, "it's only available at the winery." I'm most proud of these wines. The harder they are to find, the more personal a treasure they become.

That's the best part about touring wineries you're not familiar with: chances are no one else is either.

I started my research in Pennsylvania with Presque Isle Wine Cellars. Owners Doug and Marlene Moorhead and Marc Boettcher helped define the region I would include in this book. These three wealths of knowledge aided in my decision to include the North Shore wineries of Ontario, because they share a similar climate and growing season with the South Shore.

Once on the wine trail, I found that since wineries on all sides of the lake (and those smack in the middle) share much the same growing season, they produce very similar wines.

Of course, each winery has its own style, but the wineries all use fruit from the same region, giving the wines a regional character.

With this in mind, I have included only wineries that fall in Lake Erie's climate-moderated area, hence those wineries sharing in this regional character.

The book is intended to be a guide to every winery within the various Lake Erie viticultural regions. Along the south shore of the lake lies the Lake Erie Appellation that stretches from Buffalo in the northeast to Toledo in the southwest. Within it is the Grand River Valley sub-appellation. Then, along the lake's northern shore in Ontario lies the distinct Lake Erie North Shore and Pelee Island Viticultural Areas.

I've broken the Lake Erie Appellation on the south shore into sub-regions for the sake of day- or weekend-tripping, only because the drive from Buffalo to Toledo is a long one, and there are too many wineries in between to visit in one day. Or two. Or even three.

The wineries are organized in regional chapters so that you'll be able to go to one area and enjoy the wineries and other activities in the region. And, you can spend your time having fun, rather than flipping through the book to find adjacent wineries.

I've included listings of restaurants, bed and breakfasts and other accommodations, and regional attractions at the end of each section. Each listing has been personally recommended by the wineries for inclusion in the book. I took their word for it during my research travels, and never was I let down.

Lastly, at the end of each winery's chapter you will find a recipe. Some of these recipes are directly from the winemakers' kitchens. Others are from mine. I am excited to include many recipes from Mr. Brandt Evans, executive chef at Kosta's restaurant in Cleveland.

I had the pleasure of dining at Kosta's during the course of my research and every bite was exceptional. Evans is one of the top chefs in the region, and I encourage you to stop at his restaurant as you're driving through Cleveland. And better yet, enjoy all of these recipes in your own home with a bottle of Lake Erie wine.

This region's wine industry is blessed with some of the most gracious people I've ever met. As I toured through each winery, I was afforded the opportunity to meet the owners and winemakers and hear their highly personal stories. So much insight, so much patience, so much passion filled these men and women.

Even in the heart of harvest, these kind souls made time to speak with me about their lives and their loves. They stood patiently by as I carefully took notes and snapped photos. They offered me meals and places to stay when they found out that I was on a week-long road-trip. They welcomed me into their own homes and met with me on their days off. These are true saints, who with their artful skills are making wines that meet and, in some cases, exceed the quality wines we've all grown accustomed to from western Europe and California.

Through my research on this, the second regional winery guide in the *Discovering Wineries* series, I found superb wines that will continue to excite me for years to come. I truly hope you will share my sense of adventure and search out these wineries. I guarantee you will return home having found some new favorite wines. The trick then is finding a place to put them all!

Kevin Atticks

December 1999

Enjoy!

Lake Erie's Viticultural Regions

Wine grapes are grown in most parts of the world, but they excel in some regions due to specific land and climate conditions. When a particular region is found to be suitable for growing wine grapes, and it is distinct from other regions, it is designated an official viticultural area. Most areas are so small that they are contained within one or two counties, perhaps only within a particular valley.

Places like Napa Valley, Sonoma's Russian River Valley, Long Island in New York, and the Loire Valley in France are all specific viticultural areas. Their conditions may differ vastly from other viticulture areas in the immediate region.

Since Lake Erie is the shallowest of the Great Lakes, its warm surface temperatures late in the season allow even late-ripening grapes the time they need to mature.

This "lake effect" can be described as the moderation of climate throughout the year due to the presence of a large body of water. This allows growers in the region to plant *vinifera* grape varieties (like Cabernet Sauvignon) in seemingly strange locations (like Amherstburg, Ontario) with favorable results.

Lake Erie American Viticultural Area

The Lake Erie American Viticultural Area (A.V.A.) was designated in 1983 and is the only multi-state viticultural area in the the United States, making it truly unique among other American viticultural areas.

Running roughly from Buffalo in the northeast to Toledo in the southwest, the Lake Erie A.V.A. is also one of the largest designated areas in the United States. The A.V.A. encompasses the United States' Lake Erie Islands including South, Middle and North Bass Islands. Due to the lake's moderating effects, the potential for winter vine death is lessened, although the region is still at a higher risk than most.

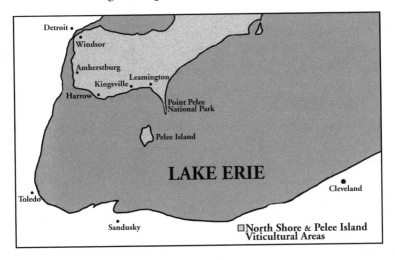

Pelee Island Viticultural Area

The Pelee Island Viticultural Area covers only the island itself. Located 15 miles off the Canadian coast in Lake Erie, Pelee Island's unique climate is excellent for grape production. As Canada's southernmost grape-growing region, the island benefits from the country's longest growing season.

Lake Erie North Shore Viticultural Area

This region, located in southwestern Ontario, is Canada's southernmost mainland grape-growing region. Including Essex, Kent and Elgin counties, this designated region affords Ontario the opportunity to make consistently excellent *vinifera* varieties and its now famous ice wine.

Quality Alliances

It's all about gaining respect. The biggest uphill battle developing wine regions must face is gaining respect from "outside" the wine community. Lake Erie's wine regions are far from new. At one time, Ohio's was the premier wine industry in the nation. Much has changed and now California reigns king.

It is entirely possible to walk into your local wine store and find absolutely no regional wine. Why? Everyone knows California, Washington and Oregon. Wines from these regions are not a hard sell. Put a bottle of Harpersfield Chardonnay next to a bottle of Kendall Jackson Reserve Chardonnay and see what happens.

Kendall Jackson wins, hands down. Is it better than the Ohio-born Harpersfield? No. Huge production, great press coverage and personal recommendations from friends will have most people reach for a California wine without thought. A fear of the unknown thwarts the sale of regional wines.

Two groups in the Lake Erie region are fighting their way onto the shelves and into the minds of consumers who might otherwise not pay attention.

On the American side of the lake, certain wine producers from New York, Pennsylvania and Ohio have formed the Lake Erie Quality Wine Alliance (LEQWA) to help gain respect both in and outside the region.

This is a members-only organization. The current members in-

clude wineries from New York, Pennsylvania and Ohio. They may accept or deny application by other wineries based on questions of quality, practices, or use of inferior grape varieties.

On the marketing front, LEQWA members have begun offering "Reflections of Lake Erie" wines, meant to showcase the region's quality winemaking and grape-growing. These wines tend to be blends, but are standouts as far as quality and taste are concerned. LEQWA has specified which grapes may be used in this wine, ensuring a minimal standard among all member wineries.

In Ontario, the Vintners Quality Alliance was formed in 1988 to set standards for the industry's wine.

These standards are rigorous and are used to classify wines worthy of VQA approval. According to official VQA rules:

- Wines must be made from classic *vitis vinifera* varieties such as Chardonnay, Pinot Noir, or Riesling, or from preferred hybrids.
- For varietal designation, wine must contain at least 85 percent of the variety named on the label, and must exhibit the dominant character of that variety.
- All grape varieties must reach a specified minimum level of natural sugar at the time of harvest – levels are set for vineyard-designated and estate-bottled wines, as well as dessert and ice wine.
- Wines described as estate-bottled must be made from 100 percent grapes owned or controlled by the winery in a viticultural area.
- If a particular vineyard designation is used, the site must be within a recognized viticultural area and all (100 percent) grapes must come from the designated vineyard.

Not all Ontario wines qualify for VQA declaration, and it is not always possible to taste a difference between the two. Look for the VQA approval on a wine's label or cap, but do not be afraid to try (or buy) unclassified wines.

Things to Know Before You Go!
(or, things I learned while writing this book!)

1. Give yourself ample time and don't schedule anything else to do the day of your visits. The whole idea of a winery is to stop in, talk, tour, and try some wine (and hopefully *BUY, BUY, BUY* when you find something you like!!). The people who greet you in the winery more than likely either own the wineries or make the wine, so spend some time talking and asking questions. You might even make some new friends.

2. Dress comfortably. None of the wineries are formal. Or even semiformal. Plus, it's probably not a bad idea to prepare for the sudden storms that whip up on and around Lake Erie.

3. Bring friends and family along. It's much more fun to visit the wineries in small groups. Kids are welcome, too (and some wineries even have fresh grape juice – *free for kids!*).

4. Don't be afraid to try all the wines. Maybe you only like reds. Maybe you only like whites. Maybe you only like Dr Pepper. Even though you may think you only like one type of wine, try all the wines available for tasting – you may find that your tastes have evolved. Keep an open mind. Besides, many wineries offer free tastings (or charge a nominal fee) so it's no loss to you!

5. Take notes. I've included a portion of each winery's wine list when in each chapter. The rest is up to you. Don't worry about wine lingo. If a wine smells like pears, pineapples, or blackberries, say so. On the flip-side, if it tastes like diesel fuel, potting soil, or a wet saddle, say so – you may be on to something! It's not necessary to like every wine tried, but it's a good idea to record your likes and dislikes for future reference. Use the space under the recipes and in the back of the book for your own notes!

6. Bring cash (although most take personal checks and credit, too!) to purchase your favorites. You'll probably find something at each winery that grabs your attention. Plus, once you see the beyond reasonable prices of some of Lake Erie's wines, you'll be making room in your car's trunk before you even reach for your wallet.

7. Plan on buying at least one bottle of wine at each winery. Most of the wineries covered in this book are small, and they count on tasting room sales to make money. All have wine priced under $10 so consider it a common courtesy to purchase a bottle, although I can almost guarantee you'll find something worth buying at each!

8. Take advantage of the local attractions. Just because the winery is a little out of the way doesn't mean it's in the middle of nowhere. I've listed some areas of interest at the end of each section, but don't just take my word for it. Call ahead or ask each winery when you arrive, to get local attraction suggestions. They would be more than happy to do so.

9. Bring your camera. Many of these wineries are located in unbelievably gorgeous settings. Snap some photos as you travel through the region – you'll have memories and some new art to frame!

10. Pace yourself and don't overdo it. If you're going to hit a few wineries in one day, make sure you stop to eat in between, lest you walk into the next winery with blurry eyes. It's always a good idea to pack a picnic lunch, and most wineries have picnic areas where you're free to munch.

11. ENJOY YOURSELF!! The best part about touring the wineries is meeting fun people and tasting their spectacular wines. As a friend once told me, "I've never had a bad wine with friends." I agree, and I hope you will too!

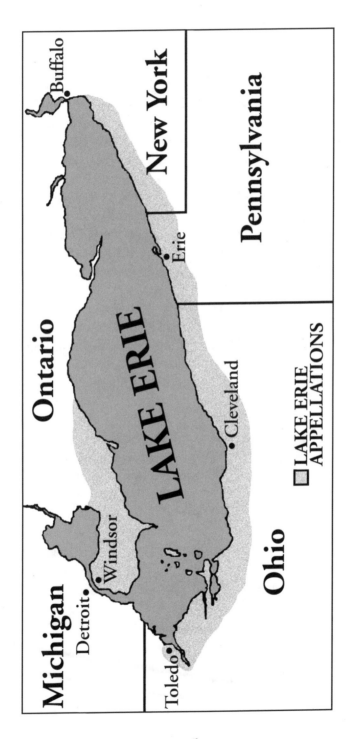

Eastern Region

Wine adds greatly
to the joy of living.

— Napoleon

Lake Erie's Eastern Region

This region stretches from Buffalo, New York in the northeast, to Erie, Pennsylvania, just southeast of the New York border. With so many non-wine attractions in and in-between these cities, this region, though small, warrants an entire weekend – or even longer.

From Presque Isle State Park in downtown Erie to the Chautauqua Institution south of Buffalo, there are both education and fun things to do for all the family.

That is – all while enjoying the wines produced along the lake. Most of the wineries fall along Rt. 20, so they're all within easy reach of the main roads. There are two main groups of wineries, which aids greatly when planning daily wine tours.

In New York, most of the wineries are situated near Westfield and Fredonia. Both towns offer main street shopping and fine bed and breakfast accommodations, as well as historic and cultural attractions to keep you busy when taking a break from the wine trail.

In Pennsylvania, all of the region's wineries fall in and around the town of North East, in between Erie and the New York border. This town is this region's mecca for grape-growing. Home of Welch's, maker of grape juice and jelly, North East hardly has room for anything but acres of Concord and Niagara grapes. Hillsides, valleys and even front yards are lined with these grapes.

The area's winemakers have found room to grow *vinifera* and hybrid vines, but the vast majority of the area's planting is *labrusca*.

Neither New York nor Pennsylvania wineries may, by law, charge for wine tastings. This allows you to freely taste small samples of many of each winery's wines, which is helpful when deciding what wines you'll take home with you!

As you travel along I-90 and Rt. 20, you'll see many beautiful sights. Have your camera ready for some of the wide-open views of Lake Erie that are provided by Rt. 20's various inclines. These beautiful vistas will complement the admirable wines you're sure to find on the road between the two great cities of Buffalo and Erie.

ARROWHEAD
WINE CELLARS

Founded:	1999
Owners:	Nick Mobilia & Patrick Murphy
Winemaker:	Jeff Murphy
Address:	12073 E. Main Road
	North East, PA 16428
Phone:	(814) 725-5509
Hours:	Monday - Saturday 10 p.m. to 6 p.m.
	Sunday 12 p.m. to 5 p.m.
Annual production:	3,000 cases
Price range of wines:	$6.99 - $12.99 US
Amenities available:	Wheelchair accessible, restrooms, adjoining Mobilia Farm Market.

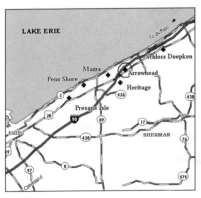

Directions:

Take exit 12 off I-90 to Route 20. The winery is located one block east of I-90 on Route 20. Arrowhead will be on your left and is connected to Mobilia Farm. Look for signs.

From Erie/North East, to east on Rt. 20 and look for Mobilia Farms on your right just before I-90.

Nick Mobilia, owner of Mobilia Farm Market in North East, had a lot of grapes – about 100 acres of them – with nowhere to send them. This, combined with his interest in wine, led him to become partners with friend Patrick Murphy and open one of Pennsylvania's newest wineries.

Arrowhead Wine Cellars, just in its infancy, has opened its door to wine lovers right next to the famous Mobilia Farm Market. From the beginning, this was a father-son venture with a lot of potential.

Jeff Murphy, son of co-owner Patrick, plays the part of winemaker at Arrowhead. He learned his craft at Heritage Wine Cellars just across the street and at a well-known Finger Lakes winery. Adrian Mobilia, son of co-owner Nick, is the vineyard manager. With all this experience, you'd never know Jeff and Adrian were each only in their early 20s.

"It was good to start this by myself," Jeff says surely, knowing that it's much easier to start things off right at the beginning rather than

Arrowhead's retail store connected to Mobilia Farm Market.

take over the job from someone else.

"Plus, we're very 'change' oriented," Jeff says. Arrowhead is planning to expand – soon. Very head-strong, yet outgoing and friendly, Jeff carries a lot of his father in him.

Take a tour of the winery, located just behind the tasting room, and you'll see how cramped the operation is already! Plans include adding storage space behind the existing winery as well as expanding the production area.

"We want to do it right," says Nick Mobilia. He thinks it's wise to grow all their own grapes, because they can have complete control over the quality of the fruit. With these four partners involved in the winery, they should have no problems with success.

"We all have to pool our knowledge, energy and resources to make the best products," adds Nick.

As for the wines, Jeff knows what he wants and he's already producing fine wines.

Currently Arrowhead is offering about ten wines, most from native and hybrid grapes. Jeff intends to add Cabernet Franc and Riesling to the line-up and has even more wines in mind for the future.

"We'll have champagne in five years," he says while reviewing his wine list.

*U*niquities:

- *Newest winery in Pennsylvania.*
- *Youngest winemaker in the region.*
- *Good variety of wines.*

The name Arrowhead Wine Cellars was chosen because Native American arrowheads have been surfacing in the vineyards for years. This honor has led to the naming of Buffalo Blush, one of their best-selling wines.

Be sure to follow Arrowhead's progress as it reaches its goals and sets new ones in the coming years. These four men have great interest in their jobs and the passion to back it up.

Wine Selections:

Delaware: Semi-dry, crisp and balanced white wine.

Buffalo Blush: Fruity blend of grape varieties with great berry aromas.

Chambourcin: Dry, oak-aged with scents of currants and black cherries.

Cherry Wine: 100% pure Pennsylvania cherries!

Mushroom, Asparagus Strudel

Ingredients: (As is, this recipe makes 10 servings)
2 tbsp butter
2 oz shallots, minced
1 tbsp garlic cloves, minced
1 lb shitake mushrooms, sliced
1/2 lb asparagus tips, blanched and sliced lengthwise
3 oz Arrowhead Delaware (or other dry or semi-dry white wine)
2 oz goat cheese
2 tbsp herb mixture (chives, dill, Italian parsley), chopped finely
6 phyllo sheets

Sweat the shallots and garlic in butter until translucent. Add mushrooms and continue to sweat. Deglace pan with white wine and cook until there's no more moisture. Fold goat cheese, mixed herbs and asparagus tips into mushroom filling. Chill mixture.

Prepare the strudel by stacking three sheets of phyllo dough, spraying each layer with a vegetable spray. Then place chilled mixture along the edge of the dough and roll up tightly. Bake strudel at 350 until golden brown.

Serve with Arrowhead's Chambourcin.

(This recipe was submitted by Brandt Evans, executive chef at Kosta's restaurant in Cleveland, Ohio.)

BLUEBERRY SKY FARM WINERY

Founded:	1997
Owners:	Rosalind & Don Heinert
Winemaker:	Don Heinert
Address:	10243 NE Sherman Road
	Ripley, NY 14775
Phone:	(716) 252-6535
WWW/E-mail:	www.lakeside.net/bsfw, bsfw@lakeside.net
Hours:	Monday - Saturday 10 a.m. to 6 p.m.
	Sunday 12 p.m. to 5 p.m.
Annual production:	700 cases
Price range of wines:	$5.00 - $10.00 US
Amenities available:	Wheelchair accessible, restroom.

Directions:
Take exit 12 off I-90. Go east one block and turn right on Gulf Road. Go up the hill and turn left at first stop sign onto Kerr Road. Go two miles on NY Rt. 6. The winery is on the right directly across from the S. Ripley Fire Hall.

When you pull into the Heinerts' driveway, you'll see why they picked this location: it's beautiful. A big open field sits to the left and the winery's on the right. Should you expect a formal tasting room? Not at all. Consider this an extension of Don and Rosalind's home.

"We're a small family-operated winery," says Rosalind. That's the way she and Don planned it: small and family-oriented. They believe their wines are good for any occasion and since they've got some unique varieties of wines and vinegars, their winery is a welcome addition the region's industry.

When Don is not experimenting with new wine varieties, he's works as a veterinarian focusing on alternative medicine. Very

Blueberry Sky's signs flag down both berry and wine lovers.

friendly and knowledgeable, Don has a great time with both his interesting professions. While this seems like a lot to juggle, Don looks to the wine as a hobby, a source of enjoyment. Plus, it's a family affair, so when not caring for the animals, Don is spending quality time with the family in the winery.

"This is a hobby gone astray," says Rosalind as she sits among Blueberry Sky's twenty-some wines. Not bad for a hobby! The Heinerts have worked hard to come up with different styles of wine to please all kinds of people.

For one thing, their variety of wines stretch the comfort zone of first-time tasters.

Some, like the onion and garlic wines, may find a happy home in the kitchen, while the fruit wines make great picnic companions. They offer some wines you'll almost never see anywhere else: rhubarb and jalapeño just to name a few. Even more unique are some of the wines in the works: tomato, cranberry, cucumber and maybe even pineapple. Many of Blueberry Sky's fruit wines come in dry and sweet versions, so you can pick the style you like best.

Rosalind and Don encourage their customers to sample all of their wines. "Try whichever wines you like," says Rosalind, pointing to the wine list.

Apparent at Blueberry Sky is the care put into the operation by the Heinerts. When they bought the land a few years back, Don's hobby was about to explode into a commercial winery.

*U*niquities:

- *Only non-grape winery in entire the region.*
- *Crazy, but wonderful, wine list including garlic, onion, strawberry and dandelion.*

"Once we had the farm, we had the fruit," says Don, who knew his winemaking hobby was about to slip way out of control. "There was nothing stopping the winery." And there seems to be nothing obstructing the Heinert's mission of creating and selling wonderful – and very unique – fruit and vegetable wines.

Wine Selections:

Dry Blueberry: Tastes like a dry red wine, with blueberry aromas.
Sweet Elderberry: Very berry! Unique wine variety.
Plum: Well, plummy! Great match with spicy Asian food.
Garlic Wine: Just a splash and your meal will improve ten-fold!

The Heinerts' Jalepeño Chili

Ingredients:

1 lb sweet Italian sausage cut into one inch lengths	1 cup chopped fresh parsley
1/4 cup olive oil	2 tbsp tomato paste
2 cups chopped onions	6 tbsp best quality chili pepper
6 cloves garlic minced	3 tbsp ground cumin
2 lbs ground beef chuck	2 tbsp dried oregano
2 green bell peppers, chopped	1 tbsp dried basil
2 red bell peppers, chopped	2 tbsp salt
6 fresh jalepeño peppers	2 lb ripe plum tomatoes, quartered
3 35-oz Italian plum tomatoes	sour cream
1 cup jalepeño wine	sliced scallions
	grated cheese

Place a large, heavy skillet over medium heat, and cook sausages until brown. Remove and drain sausages.

Heat oil in skillet, add onions, and cook garlic for five minutes until it's just about wilted. Raise the heat to medium, cook ground chuck. Add drained sausages, bell pepperss and onions to pot.

Cook for about ten minutes.

Remove skillet from stove. Add drained tomatoes, wine, parsley, tomato paste and all herbs and spices. Then, return skillet to heat, add fresh tomatoes and cook for ten minutes.

Garnish with sour cream, sliced scallions and grated cheese.

Makes 8-10 portions.

(This recipe was submitted by Rosalind Heinert of Blueberry Sky Farm Winery.)

PREMIUM

Heritage

Wine Cellars

PENNSYLVANIA TABLE WINE

Blueberry Wine

SELECTION

HERITAGE
WINE CELLARS

Founded:	1978
Owners:	Robert and Beverly Bostwick
Winemaker:	Robert Bostwick
Address:	12162 East Main Road
	North East, PA 16428
Phone:	(814) 725-8015, (800) 747-0083
WWW:	www.heritagewine.com
Hours:	Monday - Thursday 9 a.m. to 6 p.m.
	Friday - Saturday 9 a.m. to 7 p.m.
	Sunday 10 a.m. to 6 p.m.
	Winter hours may vary.
Annual production:	3,500 cases
Price range of wines:	$5.99 - $24.99 US
Amenities available:	Wheelchair accessible (winery), full-service restaurant, restrooms.

Directions:

Take exit 12 from I-90 and go east on Rt. 20 for one block. Heritage will be on your right. Look for the big hanging barrel and winery sign.

From Erie/North East, go east on Rt. 20. Heritage will be on your left just before I-90.

After walking through the giant wine barrel that marks the winery's entrance, you enter the restored 18th-century barn now known as Heritage Wine Cellars. Inside, a small, dark tasting room greets customers with gifts and a two-sided bar covered in wine.

That's not an exaggeration, either. Heritage Wine Cellars is home to nearly 50 wines – all of which line the bar for you to taste. Once up to the bar, grab a cup and help yourself to as many of the wines as you'd like to try.

Owners Robert and Beverly Bostwick allow customers to self-serve one-ounce samples of their wines, the idea being the more you try, the more you buy. There's no worry, though – you'll find something that fits your taste.

With so many wines, the Bostwicks have to juggle resources to keep everything in production at once. They produce over nine

A stroll through the Heritage's barrel will lead to a plethora of wines.

sparkling wines, alone! Heritage's specialty wines include all types of fruit wines – from blueberry to elderberry – and blends like Sangria, Holiday Spice and Dutch Apple Spice. The "Vintner's Wines" section of the wine list includes traditional *vinifera* like Cabernet Franc and Sauvignon and a late-harvest Vidal.

"Nobody makes a finer wine than Mother Nature," says Robert, who says good wine starts in the vineyard. With over 200 acres of grapes under the Bostwick's management, they have lots of choices.

The farm was bought in 1805 by Harvey Hall, great-great-grandfather of Robert Bostwick. Originally a fruit farm, Bostwick's grandfather, Kenneth Bostwick, converted the crop to grapes and so the Heritage winemaking tradition began.

Much has changed since 1805. Heritage is now supported by a fully-automated bottling line that can bottle nearly 1,000 cases daily if need be. This will be handy, as the winery's sales grew 400 percent in 1998, according to Robert Bostwick.

They're so confident of their product, the Bostwicks have placed an unconditional guarantee behind their wines.

If you don't get a chance to tour the winery, take a few minutes to see the video-tour Robert and a friend compiled a few years ago. It walks you through Heritage's winemaking process all the way from grapevine to tasting room.

*U*niquities:

- *Enormous range of wines and styles.*
- *Full-service restaurant with a grand view of Heritage's vineyards and of Lake Erie.*

After trying all the wines, take a walk upstairs to "The Gathering," the Bostwick's full-service restaurant. The rustic facility sports an outdoor deck overlooking vineyards and Lake Erie, providing a wonderful atmosphere for a late-afternoon meal.

There is no sign that the Bostwick's long winemaking tradition is coming to an end. Their two sons, Matthew and Joshua, are growing into the family business as Robert teaches them more and more about the winemaking process. The tradition is destined to continue.

Wine Selections:

White Riesling: A traditional favorite, very dry and European-styled.
Fredonia: Flowery and fruity. Great sipping red.
Dark Cherry: Truly a bowl of cherries. Not too syrupy-sweet, either!
Cold Goose: a sparkling Concord wine. Just like jam, with bubbles.

Recipe

Kevin's Honey-Baked Chicken

Ingredients:
Boneless, skinless chicken breasts
Honey
Apples (your choice - red, yellow or green all work)
Cinnamon

THIS IS A "FUTZ" RECIPE: Futz with the ingredient amounts until you are satisfied. There is hardly any preparation involved, making this a quick, easy meal. I enjoy serving this in the fall and winter because it makes the whole house smell so sweet.

Thaw as many chicken breasts as there are mouths to feed. Once defrosted, put the chicken in a bowl and pour honey over it.

Preheat the oven to 350 degrees.

Let the chicken marinate for 10 minutes, rotating and flipping the chicken a few times so that every side of every piece has been marinated.

Take a appropriately sized baking pan and pour the honey so that it thinly coats the bottom of pan.

Wash the apples and thinly slice them, leaving the skin on. Once sliced, lay the apples atop the honey in the pan, making a bed for the chicken. Place the chicken on the sliced apples, and pour the remaining marinade over the meat.

Sprinkle with a bit of cinnamon. Don't overdo it!

Place pan in the oven and let cook for 20 minutes, checking frequently to make sure it's not overcooking.

Serve with a side of rice, noodles or some other simple side dish.

Serve with Heritage Fredonia or White Riesling.

(This recipe was submitted by the author.)

JOHNSON ESTATE
VINEYARDS & WINERY

Founded:	1961
Owners:	Johnson Family
Winemaker:	Mark Lancaster
Address:	Route 20, West Main Road
	Westfield, NY 14787
Phone:	(716) 326-2191
WWW/E-mail:	www.johnsonwinery.com, jwinery@cecomet.net
Hours:	Daily 10 a.m. to 6 p.m.
Annual production:	15,000 cases
Price range of wines:	$6.45 - $15.42 US
Amenities available:	Wheelchair accessible, restroom.

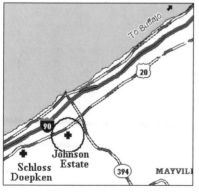

Directions:

Take exit 60 off I-90 and go south on Rt. 394 to Westfield. Turn right on Rt. 20 west. Go two miles and winery will be on your left.

Johnson Estate Vineyards and Winery has drawn many customers simply out of curiosity. The bright red building, sitting hardly a car's length off Rt. 20, is just two miles west of Westfield. You would easily pass by the building without stopping – unless you catch a glimpse of the large sign indicating the winery's identity.

Once parked and inside the winery, you will be greeted by the winery's friendly staff. Of course, when you're welcomed by free samples of wine, it's hard to not feel at home. Once you try some of Johnson's wine, you'll feel comfortable, relaxed, and delighted that you stopped by.

One hundred and ten acres of grapes are planted behind the winery with 30 more in the works. "We're planning on expanding,"

Johnson Estate's sign reading "Bonded Winery" yells a welcome call to passers-by.

declares winemaker Mark Lancaster, who says the winery has grown every year since 1991.

The vineyards yield over 400 tons of grapes every year. This amazing amount of grapes is more than the winery can use, so Johnson sells a portion to locals upon harvest.

"Yet, we've only raised our prices once in ten years," says Mark, noting the exceptional deals Johnson offers.

In fact, the most interesting aspect of the winery happens to be its exceptionally priced wines. Some regional favorites, like Niagara, Seyval and Vidal are familiar sights on Johnson's wine list. But, it's the ones like Aurora Blanc and Ives – not standards at most other wineries – which have carved out a niche for Johnson.

Johnson's Liebeströpfchen white wine, loosely translated as "Little Love Drops" in German, is an intensely rich, late-harvest Delaware wine that would be a perfect end to a filling meal.

The wine is not the only attraction at Johnson. Guided vineyard tours aboard a horse-drawn carriage leave the winery every Friday, Saturday and Sunday. You can hear the history of the vineyards and winery, and learn a lot about grape growing, all from a front-row seat.

Johnson is the oldest estate winery in New York State, meaning it uses only grapes grown

*U*niquities:

- *Oldest estate-bottled winery in New York.*
- *Classic traditional wines like Ives Noir and Delaware.*

on-site. Not many wineries can claim to be estate-bottled, and even fewer can profess to being the oldest in a state with as many wineries as New York. This places Johnson at the top of a very noble and elite list of wineries.

This winery is definitely worth the turnaround if you happen to drive past it. You will not be disappointed by the warm welcome you'll be given at Johnson Estate Vineyards and Winery.

Wine Selections:

Aurora Blanc: A bit spicy with mild fruit.
Delaware: Made from only the best bunches and free-run juice.
Ives Noir: Semi-sweet and deeply red "social," not dinner, wine.
Liebeströpfchen: Perfectly sweet, match with pies and chocolates.

ecipe

Brandt's Poached Asian Pears

Ingredients:
4 Asian pears, peeled and cored
1 1/2 cups chopped walnuts
4 cups Chevre cheese
2 cups heavy whipping cream
1 tbsp garlic, minced
1/2 cup chives
1/2 cup dill
1 pint fresh raspberries
1 btl Johnson Estate Ives Noir (or other sweet red or port wine)
1 sprig thyme
2 ea shallots, sliced
2 cups granulated sugar
Johnson Estate Chancellor Noir or other red wine

Poach the peeled and cored pears in red wine until they are red in color. Set them aside to cool.

Walnut Chevre Mousse
Whip the chevre cheese until soft. Whip the heavy cream until medium peak. Fold the cheese into the cream along with the garlic, chives and dill. When ready, fill the center of the hollow pears with the mousse.

Sauce
Reduce the port in a pot along with the thyme and shallots until you have half of what you started with. Completely dissolve the sugar into the reduction and place it into an ice bath. As the sauce cools, slowly add in the raspberries.

Serve with Johnson Estate Ives Noir or port.

(This recipe was submitted by Brandt Evans, executive chef at Kosta's restaurant in Cleveland, Ohio.)

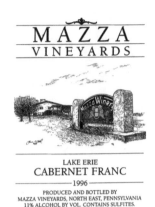

LAKE ERIE
CABERNET FRANC
1996

PRODUCED AND BOTTLED BY
MAZZA VINEYARDS, NORTH EAST, PENNSYLVANIA
11% ALCOHOL BY VOL. CONTAINS SULFITES.

MAZZA VINEYARDS

Founded:	1973
Owners:	Robert and Kathleen Mazza
Winemaker:	Gary Mosier
Address:	11815 East Lake Road
	North East, PA 16428
Phone:	(814) 725-8695
WWW/E-mail:	www.mazzawines.com
Hours:	July - Aug: Monday - Saturday 9 a.m. to 8 p.m.
	Sept - June: Monday - Saturday 9 a.m. to 8 p.m.
	Sunday 12 p.m. to 4:30 p.m. year round
Annual production:	10,500 cases
Price range of wines:	$5.80 - $12.95 (premium wines up to $49.00) US
Amenities available:	Picnic area, restrooms.

Directions:

From Buffalo, take exit 11 off I-90 and go north on Rt. 89. Go through North East and turn right on Rt. 5. The winery will be on your right.

From Erie and North East, take Rt. 5 east. Look for the winery on the right.

Walking up the stairs to Mazza's entrance, you notice more hints of Italian than just the name. The building exhibits an obvious Mediterranean influence. It's entirely intentional: Bob Mazza was born and raised in Italy before moving to America.

Mazza says his goal is to make good, drinkable wines and to gain international recognition. Maybe it's the Italian in him, but he's well on his way.

Mazza wines are generally fresh, fruity and inexpensive: just three of their wonderful aspects. The table wines are all very well made and perfectly complement any family-style meal. The Cayuga is like no other; very delicate and much tamer than some of the region's other Cayugas. The Cabernets Franc and Sauvignon and Mazza's Chambourcin and Chardonnay wines are all very respectable, while the ice wine is a treat that rarely lasts more than a few weeks on the shelves, due to its immense popularity.

Mazza's sign is just the first indication of the Mediterranean style you'll find inside.

Mazza's fruit wines are a lot of fun. The peach, spiced apple, strawberry, cherry, pear, and raspberry wines can make anyone wish it was summer again! The sparkling wines – including a sparkling Riesling – are very nice, and very affordable.

The winery is very large, but you soon see how precisely Mazza's mind works. The winery has one of the only centrifuges in the East, used to clarify and filter the wines to the purest degree. Mazza also produces grape juice that is sold to regional winemakers who swamp the winery at harvest time.

If you'd like detailed information about the winery, ask about the guided tour that ends with a slide show in the cellar. You'll hear a brief history of Mazza Vineyards while seeing photos from years past.

Bob Mazza is very supportive of the region's grape-growing and winemaking industries. Rather than settling on the success he's had at his Mazza Vineyards, Bob Mazza has also become part-owner of Penn Shore Winery. He sees the two wineries' styles as very different, so he's not really competing with himself.

"I could retire right now," says Mazza, referring to his own winery's success. So, why doesn't he? Mazza enjoys the winery too much to separate himself from the business anytime soon.

*U*niquities:

•*Light, fun sparkling wines.*
•*Informative tour and slide presentation of the winery and its proceses.*

Good thing, too, because he's the knowledge behind Mazza Vineyards.

Mazza Vineyards is not all work. "Employees must wash their feet before returning to wine cellar," announces a sign hanging above the entrance to Mazza's cellar. This sums up the friendliness and sense of humor alive in the winery. Bob Mazza, along with his wife Kathleen and two children, will surely welcome you to their winery, and hold the door for you as you leave with some of their excellent wine.

Wine Selections:

Raspberry: Combo of red/black berries. Very refreshing.
Cayuga: Citrusy and fresh; smooth and delicate.
Chambourcin: Very light and spicy red wine.

 **ecipe**

Mazza's Wine & Beef Stew

2 tbsp oil
1/2 cup flour
1 1/2 lb beef stew meat

Heat oil, coat stew meat with flour and seasonings. Brown meat. Add remaning flour to pot and add:
6 cup beef broth
2 tbsp Worchestershire sauce
2 medium onions, diced
1 cup sliced mushrooms
5 carrots cut into 1/2" pieces
4-5 potatoes, diced
1 - 1 1/2 cup Mazza Commemorative Red

Simmer until vegetables are soft. Serves 6-8.

Serve with Mazza Commemorative Red

(This recipe was submitted by Denise Hall of Penn Shore Winery and Vineyards on behalf of Mazza Vineyards.)

MERRITT
ESTATE WINERY

Founded:	1976
Owners:	William and Jason Merritt
Winemakers:	Bill & Jason Merritt
Address:	2264 King Road
	Forestville, NY 14062
Phone:	(716) 965-4800, (888) 965-4800
Hours:	Monday - Saturday 10 a.m. to 5 p.m.,
	Sunday 1 p.m. to 5 p.m.
Annual production:	5,000 cases
Price range of wines:	$5.50 - $8.99 US
Amenities available:	Wheelchair accessible, restrooms, pavilion
	for rent, picnicking.

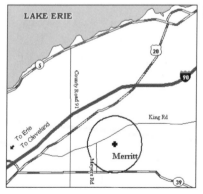

Directions:

From Buffalo, take exit 58 (Silver Creek) off I-90. Take Rt. 20 west to blinking light at Sheridan. Turn left on Center Road and follow signs to winery.

From Erie, take exit 59 (Dunkirk) off I-90. Go left on Rt. 60 to Rt. 20. Turn left on Rt. 20 to blinking light at Sheridan. Turn right on Center Road and follow signs to winery.

"Save water, drink wine," sports a T-shirt hanging in the tasting room of Merritt Estate Winery. "That pretty much sums up our attitude," says Bill Merritt, who together with his son Jason, runs the day-to-day operations of the winery.

From the looks of the place, they're doing a fine job producing and selling wine. The winery is set off the road and sits just behind the Merritt's home. Once you get down the hill to the winery, you're greeted by a large pavilion complete with an adjoining volleyball court.

"It's so much fun to be in this business now," Merritt claims. He should know: the Merritts host two major events every year – one the second weekend in June and one the second weekend in September – both of which bring hundreds of wine-lovers to the

A view of Merritt's pavilion, often rented for parties, weddings, and other "special" occasions.

winery to feast on great food and wine. Plus, the pavilion is always available for private parties, weddings, or just about any celebration that warrants an all-around good time.

Once you pass under the beautiful grape arbor to get into the winery, you'll find a spacious, bright tasting room filled with gifts, souvenirs, and of course, wine. Merritt's wine line-up includes 13 select wines ranging from a dry Chardonnay to the tangy Sangria De Marguerite, a wine dedicated to Marguerite Merritt Sample who owned the property in the 1800s.

Anyone interested in starting a winery should talk to Merritt. His sense of humor shines at the topic making light of the stress and strain of producing quality wines every year.

"I look at people like they're crazy to want to retire into this," chuckles Merritt, who says a former French intern said it best: "The work is not hard, but the day is long."

"This is not retirement!" adds Merritt, who's been working at the winery full-time for 25 years. In fact, Merritt is always looking to upgrade and improve. The future holds some great things for Merritt Estate Winery, perhaps even the addition of a restaurant.

Jason Merritt is the apprentice winemaker and a great chef, according to all sources. As he begins taking more responsibility at the winery, is Bill thinking of retiring? Not quite. He says he's in it for the long haul.

Committed to making premier quality wines, Bill Merritt speaks for the family when he says it's all about pride. "We proudly serve our wine, and we hope you're proud to serve it, too."

Uniquities:

- *Great new pavilion for events and parties.*
- *Great gift shop with fun items, inluding CDs, t-shirts, and posters.*

Wine Selections:

Chautaqua White: A semi-dry blend of grapes. Light and simple.
Chardonnay: Lightly-oaked, dry with subtle fruit.
Marechal Foch: Light red wine ideal for spaghetti *and* steak.
Edelweiss: Semi-sweet and flowery. Perfect for a romantic evening.
Sangria DeMarguerite: Very fruity and fresh with citrus and spice.

Merritt Vegetable Casserole

Ingredients:
4 medium potatoes (peeled and thinly sliced)
2 onions sliced in rings
1 cup fresh green beans cut in chunks
3 carrots sliced to 1/4" slices
1 cup Merritt Chautauqua White
1/4 cup butter, melted
1 cup small bread cubes or bread crumbs
2 cups grated cheddar cheese

Layer the vegetables from the bottom up as follows:
potatoes, onions, green beans, tomatoes, and carrots.

Pour the wine over the top and salt and pepper to taste.

Bake at 375 for 1 hour in a covered casserole. (Until vegetables are soft but crisp.)

Mix bread crumbs with butter and sprinkle grated cheese and bread mixture over casserole. Return to oven and bake for 15 additional minutes.

Serve with Merritt Chautauqua White.

(This recipe was submitted by Merritt Estate Winery.)

PENN SHORE
WINERY & VINEYARDS

Founded:	1968
Owners:	Robert Mazza, President, George W. Sceiford, Secretary-Treasurer
Winemaker:	Gary Mosier, consulting
Address:	10225 East Lake Rd (Rt 5)
	North East, PA 16428
Phone:	(814) 725-8688
Hours:	July - Aug: Monday - Saturday 9 a.m. to 8 p.m., Sunday 11 a.m. to 4:30 p.m.
	Sept - June: Monday - Saturday 9 a.m. to 5:30 p.m. Sunday 11 a.m. to 4:30 p.m.
Annual production:	6,300 cases
Price range of wines:	$5.95. - $12.95 US
Amenities available:	Wheelchair accessible, picnic tables, restrooms.

Directions:
From Buffalo and Erie, take exit 11 off I-90. Go north on Rt. 89 to Rt. 5. Turn left on Rt. 5 and go one mile. The winery will be on your left.

Penn Shore Winery & Vineyards is a very popular stop along Rt. 5 in North East. How about the hard-to-find wines they offer? Or their affordable prices?

Yes. All of the above. Penn Shore serves up a few of the usual varieties consumers have come to expect like Chardonnay and Vidal, and Baco Noir on the red side. But Penn Shore also offers Diamond and the blended wine, Kir – two of the winery's most popular items.

"We came from Erie for their Kir," says a customer who drove to the winery with five friends, all for the love of Kir. While Penn Shore is a now a leader of inexpensive fine wine, the winery's original owners had to fight to make the winery legal.

The original owners of Penn Shore spearheaded the development of Pennsylvania's Limited Winery Act. The law, which was eventually passed in 1968, allows grape growers to sell wine directly from

Penn Shore Winery & Vineyards is a haven for bus tours. If you see one coming, get in line quick!

their own retail outlet and tasting room. With the passing of this law, Penn Shore opened and began its tradition that has been continually upheld.

Bob Mazza of Mazza Vineyards bought a controlling interest in Penn Shore in 1987. With his expertise and experience in the field, Mazza breathed new life into Penn Shore and the winery has been running a brisk business ever since.

Denise Hall, Penn Shore's manager, thinks the winery has

improved over the years due the experience of all parties involved. Hall should know – she's been with Penn Shore since 1989 and has seen the winery prosper and grow through the years.

"You can still get a quality wine at a bargain price," says Hall, noting that all but the Champagne fall under $9.00. Hall does most everything at the winery from bottling and labeling, to selling the wine in the retail store.

The retail store and tasting room is huge – cavernous, in fact. It could easily accommodate a bus tour of thirsty wine lovers. The tasting bar is to the left of the retail shop, and is large and open on two sides to keep up with all the tasters.

Penn Shore offers a tour of its facilities where you can sneak a peek at the vast production facilities. When Denise gives the tour, she's very down-to-earth about technical aspects of the winery, and makes it all easy to understand.

*U*niquities:

- *Wonderful, inexpensive wines.*
- *Owners pioneered Pennsylvania's Limited Winery Act in 1968.*

When you taste Penn Shore's wines, you'll notice their simple, fruity tastes and overall quality. And when the price finally sinks in, you'll notice just how heavy they are when you buy them by the case.

Wine Selections:

Vignoles: Oaky with round fruit flavors.

Kir: A blend of Seyval, Pink Catawba and black currant.

Crystal Lake White: Very sweet "with a hint of fruitiness," says Penn Shore's brochure.

Vignoles Chicken Stew

Ingredients:
1 1/2 lbs chicken thigh or breast cut into bite size chunks
1 tbsp oil
1 medium onion chopped
1 tbsp minced garlic
2 qts water
salt and pepper to taste
4 chicken boullion cubes
2 cups sliced carrots
2 tbsp parsley
1 cup frozen peas
1/2 cup Penn Shore Vignoles
4 oz mushrooms
8 tbsp butter or margarine melted
8 tbsp flour
4 oz sour cream

In 4 qt stock pot, brown chicken pieces with onion and garlic in oil. Add water, boullion cubes and carrots. Add salt and pepper, cover and simmer for 45 minutes. Add parsley, peas, and Penn Shore Vignoles. Simmer 5 more minutes and add mushrooms. Thicken with melted butter or margarine mixed with flour. Add sour cream and adjust seasonings.

Serve with Penn Shore Vignoles.

(This recipe was submitted by Denise Hall of Penn Shore Winery & Vineyards.)

PRESQUE ISLE
WINE CELLARS

Founded:	1969
Owners:	Doug and Marlene Moorhead, Marc Boettcher
Winemaker:	Doug Moorhead
Address:	9440 Buffalo Road
	North East, PA 16428
Phone:	(814) 725-1314
WWW:	www.piwine.com
Hours:	Year-round: Monday - Friday 8 a.m. to 5 p.m.
	Sept - Oct: Monday - Saturday 8 a.m. to 6:30 p.m.
	Sunday 8 a.m. to 3 p.m.
Annual production:	2,000 cases
Price range of wines:	$5.00 - 14.00 US
Amenities available:	Wheelchair accessible, restrooms, picnic deck.

Directions:

From Buffalo, take exit 11 off I-90 and go north on Rt. 89. Turn left on Rt. 20 and Presque Isle will be on your right.

From Erie, take Rt. 20 east. Before entering North East, look for the winery on the left.

There are relatively few warm-hearted, selfless people in the wine trade who compare to Doug Moorhead, his wife Marlene and partner Marc Boettcher. Doug is known throughout the region by both commercial winemakers and home winemakers as "the" man with all the answers. Moorhead has garnered somewhat of a guru status among winemakers.

It is through their winemaking supply catalog store that Presque Isle Wine Cellars has made a nationally recognized name.

Very quick and witty, Moorhead is an inspiration to everyone he meets. Marlene's sense of humor, comforting tone and knowledgeable presence quickly make you feel at home in the winery. Marc is very involved in the Lake Erie Quality Wine Alliance (LEQWA) and holds great admiration for the region's other wineries.

The entire Presque Isle operation has taken on a friendly, educational feel. Wine and books fight for your attention in the tasting room – but in the cool, damp cellar, the wine reigns supreme. The

Presque Isle's deck sits amidst a beautiful setting of trees and a quiet stream.

tasting room is bright, and surrounded by windows overlooking the many trees and a shale stream bed that lines the property below.

As winemaker, Moorhead strives to create quality wines that appeal to the general public. While he uses only the best grapes, his style of winemaking removes much of the pretentious feel of some of the varieties.

Presque Isle's Cabernet Sauvignon is smooth, containing few tannins but lots of luscious fruit. The Carmine wine – made from a grape with a crossed heritage consisting of hybrid, *vinifera*, and yet more *vinifera* varieties – is soft and simple with soothing aromas and flavors.

As Moorhead pours wine to sample, history and anecdotes spill through his voice as fast as he can think. "I admit to being a peasant at heart," says Moorhead as he evaluates his wine with a swish and a grin. It's quickly apparent just how much information and knowledge is stored behind Moorhead's unassuming stature.

As he raises his glass – filled with a peppery Syrah jammed with fruit flavors – Moorhead describes it as "a wine for all."

Doug passionately promotes other local wineries and says they promote Presque Isle too. He assumes the ideal that common knowledge and promotion can only help the local wine industry as a whole.

*U*niquities:

- *Mail-order supplier to commercial and home winemakers throughout the region.*
- *Carmine, a luscious red wine.*

Presque Isle's vineyards include *vinifera* like Chardonnay, Cabernet Sauvignon, Cabernet Franc, Riesling and Pinot Noir, Viognier and Petit Verdot. Also planted are hybrids such as Foch, Chambourcin, Vidal and Seyval.

When driving on Rt. 20 in North East, look carefully for Presque Isle's sign, because you would not want to miss an experience with these three extraordinary people…or the artful wines they create.

Wine Selections:

Carmine: A red hybrid with full, forward fruit. Unique!
Gewürztraminer: Dry and floral. Very small production.
Cabernet Franc: Very cherry with slight tannins.

Brandt's Polenta Crusted Walleye

Ingredients:
4 6-oz walleye filets, cut
1/2 cup Thai chili sauce
4 tbsp sweet soy
1 lb butter
6 cups white wine
1/2 cup cream
6 cups dried apples - diced
3 cups cooked yucca root, diced
2 tbsp scallions - sliced
2 1/2 tbsp pickled ginger
juice from one lemon
bread crumbs
polenta /corn meal

Season the walleye and coat with polenta. Sauté with olive oil until golden brown.

Sauce
Reduce the white wine and lemon juice until there is only 4 tbsp left. Add the cream and bring to a boil. Slowly whisk in the butter until it has completely emulsified. Add pickled ginger, Thai chili sauce and sweet soy to finish.

Apple Yucca Cakes
Peel the skin from the yucca root and dice it. Place the yucca in cold, salted water and bring to a boil. Boil the yucca until it is soft, adding additional salted water when the water level drops. Sauté the cooked yucca with the apples, garlic and scallions until the mixture is almost mushy. Place in a bowl and mash. Add bread crumbs until the desired consistency is reached and form into cakes. Sauté the cakes until golden brown.

Serve with Presque Isle Gewürztraminer.

(This recipe was submitted by Brandt Evans, executive chef at Kosta's restaurant in Cleveland, Ohio.)

SCHLOSS DOEPKEN WINERY

Founded: 1980
Owners: J. Simon and Roxann Watso
Winemaker: J. Simon Watso
Address: 9177 Old Route 20
Ripley, NY 14775
Phone: (716) 326-3636
Hours: Daily, 12 p.m. to 5 p.m.
Annual production: 3,300 cases
Price range of wines: $6.50 - $27.00 US

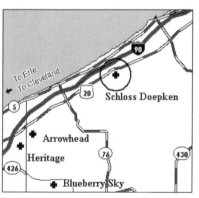

Directions:

From Buffalo, take exit 60 off I-90 and go south to Westfield. Turn right on Rt. 20 and follow until you see signs for Old Rt. 20. Turn left onto Old Rt. 20 and follow to winery.

From Erie, take exit 61 off I-90 and go south to Rt. 20. Turn left on Rt 20 until you see signs for Old Rt. 20. Turn right on Old Rt. 20 and follow to winery

This winery's name is as interesting as its wine. Owners J. Simon and Roxann Watso have been producing fine wines since 1980. And they've surely answered this question more times than they can count: What does Schloss Doepken really mean?

The German translation of Schloss is "castle" or "house," while Doepken is the maiden name of J. Simon's wife, Roxann. As wine-maker, J. Simon Watso has devoted the rest of his life to Roxann's castle.

And what a good choice that was. Schloss Doepken has become a local tradition. Located just off the current Rt. 20, the winery has seen many regular customers, but has also seen its share of out-of-towners just passing through.

"We're getting a whole lot smarter about planting grapes than every before," says Watso, referring to the region's improvement as

Sample Schloss Doepken's wines in the cozy tasting room located in the owners' home.

a whole. He says it's been a long time coming, but now most wine-growers are growing or planting *vinifera* varieties. His vineyards are filled with rows of *vinifera* and hybrid vines, cascading down the property's slope.

"Making wine is not a whole lot different than making steel," says Watso, implicating quality raw materials as the key element to both. In his case, the grapes are key. Planted in 1974, his grapes' quality is immediately noticed in his wine.

According to Watso, a wine judge once sniffed a Schloss Blanc and was enamoured with the aroma that wafted out of the glass. "That's a 100-year-old nose," said the man, attesting to the depth even of Watso's lower-priced white.

His Chardonnays, one dry and oaked, and the other semi-dry without any oak aging, are both very nice. Watso says these two wines speak well to different tastes, and he ends up selling Chardonnay to everyone. His Roxann Rouge is a tribute to his wife. If she's anything like the wine, she's a real treat.

Schloss Doepken's Cabernet Sauvignon is usually in such short supply that there's a three-bottle limit imposed to ensure it stays around a while.

As you park in front of Schloss Doepken's tasting room and retail shop, you'll notice a large,

*U*niquities:

- *Quaint location, set off old Route 20.*
- *Chautauquablümchen: the name's not the only thing unique about this wine.*

tilting tree standing alone in the house's front yard. "That's my 'bending birch,'" says Watso as he admires the tree. He says it's the only one around and that it has endured years of constant wind, giving it a slight lean.

"Hopefully someday," says Watso, as he looks up the vine-covered escarpment behind his winery, "we'll have a real Schloss for all to see." If Watso continues making quality wine, that day may come soon.

Wine Selections:

Schloss Blanc: Very smooth and elegant, a blend of past vintages.
Chautauquablümchen: "Little flower of Chautauqua." Sweet Riesling – but pink.
Roxann Rouge: Baco Noir aged four winters in oak. Very smooth.

 *ecipe*

Kevin's Grilled Herbed Portobellos

Ingredients:
1-2 portobello mushrooms for each mouth to feed
oregano, thyme, sage, garlic
parmesan cheese
Schloss Doepkin's Ripley Red

Clean mushrooms and remove stems. Pour the wine into the mushrooms' cap so that the gills are visibly moist. Add herbs and cheese at will.

Allow to marinate for at least 15 minutes before cooking. Place on the grill for 3 to 5 minutes. Don't let them burn!

Serve this as a main course with rice (over spaghetti works great, too) or as a complement to a meat dish.

Serve with Schloss Doepken's Ripley Red.

(This recipe was submitted by the author.)

1997
Vetter Vineyards
CHARDONNAY
NEW YORK STATE
Produced and Bottled by Vetter Vineyards
Westfield, New York 14787 • BW731
Alcohol 11% by Volume

VETTER VINEYARDS

Founded:	1987
Owners:	Craig Vetter
Winemaker:	Craig Vetter
Address:	8005 Prospect Road
	Westfield, NY 14787
Phone:	(716) 326-3100
E-mail:	cvett@cecomet.net
Hours:	Monday - Saturday 11 a.m. to 5 p.m.,
	Sunday 12 p.m. to 5 p.m.
Annual production:	3,000 cases
Price range of wines:	Starting at $8.00
Amenities available:	Wheelchair accessible, restroom.

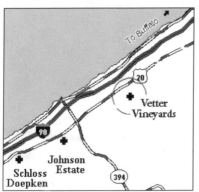

Directions:
From Buffalo and Erie, take exit 60 off I-90 and go south to Westfield. Turn left on Rt. 20 and follow to Prospect Road. Turn right on Prospect Road and you'll see the winery atop the first hill on the right.

When Craig Vetter decided to open a winery, he chose a location right on Rt. 20, Westfield's Main Street. It was a fine location with good exposure to traffic and tourists. It did, though, have the look and feel of an auto parts store: plain design and single-pane display windows from floor to ceiling.

In *Wineries of the Great Lakes,* by Joe Borrello, Vetter Vineyards' old facility was described as "more businesslike than fanciful." This worked well for Vetter for a number of years. Then, things changed.

The winery was moved.

"The winery is where it should have always been," says Vetter, with a chuckle. It is now located at his home, which happens to be where he maintains his original 22 acres of grapes. Finally, his winery is justifiably surrounded by the vineyards that have given it life

The Vetter homestead now doubles as Vetter Vineyards, complete with production facilities and tasting room.

for so long.

Attached to his house is a two-car garage, which now serves as a retail space and tasting room for the new winery. Vetter's entire 1,300 square feet of basement has been converted into the winery's production area.

Incidentally, the winery's previous residence has been renovated and is now what *it* should always have been: an auto parts store.

Trees line the driveway leading to the Vetter household and winery. On most days, the wind is blowing off the lake and up the hill-side through the vineyards, creating a constant flutter of leaves which drowns out any noise that may come from the town below.

Craig Vetter is great supporter of *vinifera* and hybrid wines. His vineyards are filled with Chardonnay, Riesling, Gewürztraminer, Cabernet Sauvignon, Chambourcin, Seyval and Vignoles.

"I grow all my own grapes and sell the excess," says Vetter. He has a prized vineyard site located on the escarpment overlooking Westfield and Lake Erie, which he first planted with *vinifera* in 1970.

Vetter Vineyards has come a long way since it first opened. Craig's winemaking techniques have evolved over the years, his vines have aged and are producing better fruit, and now he's starting anew in new,

*U*niquities:

- *New location just east of Westfield at original vineyard site.*
- *Simple, high-quality wine selection.*

yet familiar surroundings. Even if you've been to Vetter Vineyards before, now's a great time to check back in and reintroduce yourself to Vetter's variety of fine wines.

Recipe

Brandt's Scallop and Bok Choy Lasagna

Ingredients:
8 scallops
4 baby bok choy heads
4 pumpkin pasta sheets, cut into squares
1 cup shiitake mushrooms
1/2 lb balsamic red onions
2 tbsp Cherve cheese
1/2 cup tomato concasse
4 cup heavy whipping cream
2 tbsp whole grain mustard
1/2 cup capers
salt and pepper
herbs

Slice the scallops in half and sear them quickly in a pan, making sure not to overcook them. In a separate pan, sauté the mushrooms, bok choy, tomato concasse and onions. Once this is cooked, add the scallops, chevre cheese and herbs. Layer the filling with the boiled pasta squares as you would with any other type of lasagna.

Cream Sauce
Reduce cream in a pot until nappe. Add mustard and capers and season to taste.

Serve with Vetter's Chardonnay.

(This recipe was submitted by Brandt Evans, executive chef at Kosta's restaurant in Cleveland, Ohio.)

WOODBURY VINEYARDS

Founded:	1979
Owners:	Gary Woodbury
Winemaker:	Andy Dabrowski
Address:	3230 South Roberts Road
	Fredonia, NY 14063-9417
Phone:	(716) 679-9463, (888) NYS-WINE
WWW/E-mail:	www.woodburyvineyards.com,
	wv@woodburyvineyards.com
Hours:	Monday - Saturday 9 a.m. to 5 p.m.
	Sunday 12 to 5 p.m., Summers open till 8 p.m.
Annual production:	15,000 cases
Price range of wines:	$5.99 - $20.00 US
Amenities available:	Wheelchair accessible, pavilion for rent, picnic areas, restrooms.

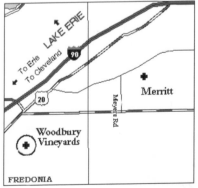

Directions:
From Buffalo and Erie, take exit 59 off I-90. Turn left on Rt. 60, then left on Rt. 20. Turn right on S. Roberts Road and follow to winery on right.

Gary Woodbury is a respectable man. He's an owner and chief operating officer of the wildly successful Woodbury Vineyards, but you'd never know it. This retired high school chemistry teacher is friendly, outgoing yet modest about his wines.

His shareholders, on the other hand, are so excited about Gary's wines that they've invested thousands of dollars in Woodbury to ensure its long-term success.

That's right: shareholders. Woodbury Vineyards went public in 1996 in order to gather immediate funds for expansion. Some of the profits of this stock offering have been put toward a new picnic pavilion, warehouse, and a fully-automated filling and bottling line.

"We made the price of the shares low to get more investors," says Gary, who looks very highly upon his shareholders. "We now have many ambassadors of our wines."

The new picnic pavilion nestled in an apple orchard now serves as

"Adopt a Barrel" has become one of Woodbury's most popular programs.

a meeting place for many organizations that hold their annual picnics at Woodbury. Complete with a sand volleyball court and a large lawn for other activities, Woodbury is a great place for private events.

Woodbury offers an "Adopt a Barrel" program through which you can become a "parent" of a new barrel full of soon-to-be-wine. When each wine in the barrel's lifetime is ready, you receive two cases. The barrel is yours once it's retired from the cellar, or you can choose to donate it back to Woodbury.

Woodbury's farm started long before the winery was even dreamed of. In 1909, the Woodbury family planted apples, cherries, peaches, pears and grapes. While these crops seem diverse, Gary's grandmother had a general farm rule: "If you have to bend over to pick it, we don't grow it."

Today, Woodbury's farm consists mostly of grapes. Riesling, Chardonnay, Merlot, Pinot Noir and Concord fill the 40 acres of vineyards. Woodbury still needs to buy grapes from local growers to support its operation.

Gary was inspired to grow *vinifera* grapes by Dr. Konstantin Frank. He, like many other growers in the region, met Dr. Frank and were convinced to try European varieties. "If I hadn't met him, we wouldn't have a winery," says Gary.

The tasting room is bright and comfortable, with windows and shelves all around. You may get to meet Petrus, Woodbury's sleek black wine cat, as she sleeps on the cash register. "If she had a nickel for every hand that passed over her...she'd be rich," Gary says.

Gary has a lot of complimentary things to say about the Lake Erie winegrowing region and he's willing to share information and give advice. Make sure you allow time to taste all of the wines and take a tour of the new facilities to see for yourself where Woodbury's been, and where it's quickly heading.

*U*niquities:

- *New pavilion on-site in apple orchard for private parties and events.*
- *Only regional winery to funded by stock offerings.*

Wine Selections:

Chardonnay: American oak aged, smooth with a crisp finish.
Seaport White: Blend of Seyval and Cayuga. Inexpensive and fruity.
Merlot: Light-bodied, oaky and dry with some cherry aromas.

Recipe

Woodbury's Chardonnay Chicken

Ingredients:
4-6 boneless chicken breasts, pounded
1/2 cup Woodbury's Chardonnay
1/4 cup lemon juice
5-6 green onions, chopped
2 cloves garlic, pressed
butter
flour

Lightly flour chicken and fry in butter until golden brown, about 5 minutes on each side. Place in warm oven. Add 3 tbsp of butter to pan. Saute onions and garlic in butter, add wine and lemon juice. Simmer on low for 5 minutes. Add chicken to sauce, cover and simmer for 5-10 Minutes. Serve with rice.

Serve with Woodbury's Chardonnay.

(This recipe was submitted by the staff of Woodbury Vineyards.)

Regional Suggestions

Restaurants:

Freeport Restaurant
Rt 5 & 89
North East, PA 16428
(814) 725-4607

Peek 'n Peak
1405 Olde Rd
Clymer, NY 14724
(716) 355-4141

Johnny B's
37 Vine St.
North East, PA 16428
(814) 725-1762

Accommodations:

Blue Heron Inn & Restaurant
10412 Main St
Findley Lake, NY 14736
(716) 769-7852

Vineyard B&B
10757 Sidehill Road
North East, PA 16428
(814) 725-8998

Brookside Manor
3728 Rt 83
Fredonia, NY 14063
(716) 672-7721

Westfield House
E. Main Road, Rt. 20
Westfield, NY 14787
(716) 326-6262

Grape Arbor Inn
51 East Main St.
North East, PA 16428
(814) 725-5522 / 8471

White Inn
Main Street, Rt 20
Fredonia NY 14063
(716) 672-2103

Local Attractions:

Pashke Mum Farm
North East, PA

Historic Railway Museum
North East, PA

Presque Isle State Park
Presque Isle State Park
P.O. Box 8510
Erie, PA 16505
(814) 833-7424

Maritime Museum
150 East Front Street
Erie, PA 16507
(814) 452-BRIG

The 1891 Fredonia Opera House
9-11 Church Street
Fredonia, NY 14063
(716) 679-1891

Lucy-Desi Museum
212 Pine Street
Jamestown, NY 14701
(716) 484-7070

Chautauqua Institution
One Ames Avenue
Chautauqua, NY 14722
(800) 836.ARTS

Central Region

*Making a good wine is a skill;
making fine wine is an art.*

— Robert Mondavi

Lake Erie's Central Region

This is the true heart of the Lake Erie Appellation. Focused in Ohio, and including Conneaut Cellars Winery in Conneaut Lake, Pennsylvania, this region is producing the finest grapes on the south side of Lake Erie. Its wineries also boast extremely varied wine lists, covering everything from DeChaunac to Agawam to Baco Noir and Pinot Noir.

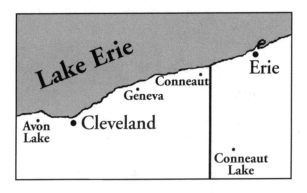

If you've never tried these varieties, here's your chance. I learned so much in this region. One of the finest Pinot Noirs I have ever tasted came from the St. Joseph Vineyard, a small, estate-bottled winery in Thompson. Who would have guessed that this delicate red grape could outdo most any other I had tried.

Markko Vineyard and Harpersfield Vineyard prove, without a doubt, that Chardonnay can thrive in northern Ohio. Any questions about the viability of *vinifera* in the region have been shattered by these three wineries.

Vinifera varietals are not the only wines excelling here. Hybrid vines are also producing superb fruit, and most every winery showcases this quality in their wines.

The demand for traditional, native wines is ever demanding. Many of the region's wineries make *labrusca* wines, while some focus entirely on them.

Focus on the Region's Newest Stars

Jerome Welliver describes himself as the CEO, winemaker and janitor of Heartland Vineyards. It's a lucky thing he is good at all of them. In the former home of Dover Vineyards, Welliver has created his new winery.

He's currently offering 15 wines, including meads (honey wine) and mead/fruit blends.

If that's not enough, Heartland is also a 1,500 square foot beer and wine-making supplier. If you're driving through Cleveland,

Heartland Vineyards resides in the old Dover winery.

swing by Heartland in Westlake to taste Welliver's new wines – who knows...you may leave with some winemaking supplies of your own.

Heartland Vineyards
24945 Detroit Road
Westlake, OH 44145
(440) 871-0700

A new winery and brewpub is opening just south of Cleveland in Berea, Ohio. Located right in Berea's main shopping district, Quarry Ridge Winery is sure to find many hungry – and thirsty – customers interested in some home-made wine and beer.

Quarry Ridge Winery
58 Front Street
Berea, OH 44017
(440) 986-2255

The soon-to-be home of Quarry Ridge Winery in Berea, Ohio.

Again, a special note of thanks to Chef Brandt Evans of Kosta's restaurant in Cleveland for graciously donating his recipes. I greatly enjoyed his restaurant and highly recommend it. Simply superb!

Biscotti Family Winery

Founded:	1995
Owners:	Joe & Larry Biscotti; Dick, Dave & Laurie McLaughlin
Winemakers:	Joe Biscotti & Larry Biscotti
Address:	186 Park Ave Conneaut, OH 44030
Phone:	(440) 593-6766
Hours:	Tuesday - Saturday 4:30 p.m. to 10 p.m.
Annual production:	1,700 cases
Price range of wines:	$9.00 - $19.00 US
Amenities available:	Wheelchair accessible, restrooms, full-service restaurant

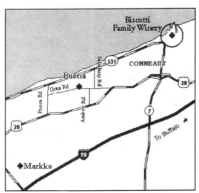

Directions:
Take the Rt. 7 exit off I-90. Go north on Rt. 7. Follow to Park Ave and turn right. Winery will be on your left.

Joe Biscotti has been in the restaurant business for most of his life. A few years ago, he expanded into the realm of winemaking. Biscotti Family Winery opened in 1995 with everything you need to have a nice time: food, wine, and more wine. The wine can be tasted in Biscotti's Italian restaurant, located just one block from Lake Erie.

New to the wine business, Joe has received a lot of support from Tony Debevc, owner of Chalet Debonné.

"I've had a lot of help from Tony," says Joe Biscotti, who is grateful for the support he's received from other wineries. He says Debevc even helps with some of the bottling.

"As far as I'm concerned, he's one of the best winemakers in the

Biscotti's quaint restaurant provides a nice atmosphere in which to discover their wine.

area. Plus, I've learned a lot about Niagara and Concord from Ed Moroski."

This is very much a boutique winery, producing only 2,000 gallons of wine a year. Biscotti has absolutely no trouble selling that small amount, though. "We sell hundreds of bottles of wine a week in the restaurant," says Joe Biscotti.

His restaurant is small, but the food is great. You can get all types of home-cooked food and you have the opportunity to pair it with your favorite Biscotti wine…or try them all till you find "the one."

All of Biscotti's wines are fun and flavorful. Joe makes an odd brew of varieties, including Merlot, Chardonnay, Concord, and Strawberry. He makes some blends, too.

The Biscotti fruit wines are very popular, and that's no surprise when you hear Joe describe them. "The strawberry is like drinking strawberry juice," adds Joe. "They love that stuff!" He also makes peach and elderberry wines to calm the fruit lover in all of us.

Biscotti's wine is made in two cellars; one in Joe's home and the other at the restaurant. Much of Biscotti's juices are bought from local growers, although some comes from out of the region.

Uniquities:

- *Great Italian restaurant right on site; perfect end to a long day of winetasting.*
- *Very good, simple wines.*

Joe is not the sole proprietor of this operation. Partners Dick, Dave and Laurie McLaughlin and Joe's son Larry are also involved in the winery.

Joe plans to expand the winery's retail space soon and intends to market his wines as the winery grows. Until then, you can find his wine at the winery and at a few select retailers in the immediate area.

If you want the full platter, get to Biscotti Family Winery to enjoy a savory meal complemented by a big round glass of Biscotti wine.

Wine Selections:

Nancy's Blush: Blend of Niagara, Concord, Catawba.
Biscotti's most popular.
Classic Pasta Red: Semi-dry old-fashioned Italian wine.
Strawberry: Strawberry essence abounds in this very berry blush.
Pinot Gris: Spicy, oaky… simply delightful.

 *ecipe*

Brandt's Field Green Salad with Ginger, Wasabi & Peanut Dressing

Ingredients:
Mesclun mix
Tofu - roughly diced

Dressing:
1 tbsp garlic, chopped
2 oz honey
1 oz peanut butter
5 oz red wine vinegar
2 oz soy sauce
2 tbsp hosin sauce
1 tbsp ginger, finely chopped
2 tbsp wasabi powder
10 oz peanut/vegetable oil
salt
white pepper
sesame seeds, white and black

Combine all of the dressing ingredients except for the oil. Then gradually incorporate the oil. Salt and pepper to taste.

Serve with Biscotti's Pinot Gris.

(This recipe was submitted by Brandt Evans, executive chef at Kosta's restaurant in Cleveland, Ohio.)

BUCCIA VINEYARD

Founded:	1976
Owners:	Fred & Joanna Bucci
Winemaker:	Fred Bucci
Address:	518 Gore Road
	Conneaut, OH 44030
Phone:	(440) 593-5976
Hours:	Open daily, except Sunday
Annual production:	2,000 cases
Price range of wines:	$5.90 - $10.00 US
Amenities available:	B&B, wheelchair accessible, restrooms, pavilion for picnicking.

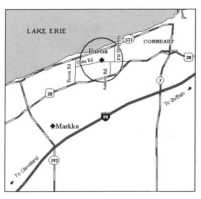

Directions:

Take Rt. 7 exit off I-90. Go north on Rt. 7 to Rt. 20. Turn left on Rt. 20 and continue to Gore Road. Turn right on Gore Road. Winery will be on the right, after the railroad tracks.

After crossing the railroad tracks, Buccia Vineyard blossoms on your right. Fred and Joanna have picked a nice location for their winery – secluded and surrounded by vineyards and apple trees. Their house looks oddly long at first – and justifiably so. Hiding inside is a winery, bed and breakfast, and tasting room.

The Buccis have done a lot to accommodate your every need when visiting their winery. There is a picnic area in front of the winery entrance, where the tables are shaded by a grape-covered arbor – perfect for a pre- or post-tasting meal. Their tasting room is equipped with a few tables and two booths if you'd like to taste in private. But that's no fun, because the Buccis are outgoing and friendly, and truly enjoy taking people on a tasting-tour of their wines.

A look at Buccia Vineyard, where you can come inside with all your bags and enjoy their bed & breakfast.

"If you don't like it, dump it – at least you've have the experience," suggests Joanna, while guiding some guests through Buccia wines. With up to twelve wines at any given time, the Buccis have a small, but complete variety to offer. The Buccis also offer wine-related books and gifts in their tasting room.

Winemaker Fred Bucci produces a few odd, lesser-known wines. Agawam, a hybrid grape, grows locally and Fred has been buying the grapes for years. "It's the only one in the country," claims Fred, who's done enough research to know that only there are only 600

Agawam vines on record in the United States, and he's buying grapes from most of them. The Agawam vineyard he's purchasing from is over 85 years old.

"I'm a home winemaker run amuck," says Fred, who has only been working the winery full-time for a few years. Prior, he juggled a job in the local government with the demands of the winery. He retired to take full advantage of the winery and B&B, expanding and improving both over the years.

Their bed & breakfast, which Fred says started as an accident, is attached to wine tasting room. "We wanted a hot tub for ourselves," he says, "so we added a room to accommodate it." Then, customers began inquiring about renting the hot tub for the evening. Fred thought it would be nice if people could then stay for the night after their wine and hot tub events. With this, the Buccis decided to venture into the B&B business.

Uniquities:

- *Bed & Breakfast connected to the winery.*
- *Some interesting wine varieties, including Agawam.*

All the Buccis need is a restaurant, and their guests would never have to leave. But then, they certainly have their hands full with the winery and B&B. Whether or not you're planning to stay in the area, stop by the winery to taste Buccia's not-so-known varieties and at least ask to see the rooms – which are just as much fun and unique as the wine.

Wine Selections:

Agawam: Fruity and semi-sweet. Made from 85-yr-old Agawam vines – possibly the only Agawam vineyard left planted in the America!

Maiden's Blush: Soft and light, with mild sweetness.

Buccia's Spinach Seyval Spread

Ingredients:
8 oz chopped spinach, thawed and drained.
1 14 oz can artichokes, drained and cut in small pieces
1 8 oz package cream cheese
1/2 cup parmesan cheese
2-4 tbsp Seyval wine (dry white)

Mix all ingredients together. Add a little garlic salt to taste. Microwave until bubbly. Serve with tortilla chips.

Serve with Buccia Seyval.

(This recipe was submitted by Joanna Bucci of Buccia Vineyard.)

River Blanc

LAKE ERIE SEMI-SWEET TABLE WINE

CHALET DEBONNÉ
VINEYARDS

Founded:	1976
Owners:	The Debevc Family
Winemaker:	Linda King
Address:	7743 Doty Road
	Madison, OH 44057
Phone:	(440) 466-3485
WWW/E-mail:	www.debonne.com
Hours:	Tuesday - Saturday 12 p.m. to 8 p.m.
	Wednesday - Friday 12 p.m. to 11 p.m.
Annual production:	26,000 cases
Price range of wines:	$5.89 - $14.00 US
Amenities available:	Wheelchair accessible, full-service grill, outdoor seating, restrooms.

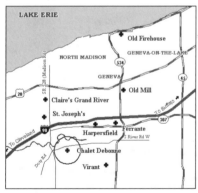

Directions:

From Cleveland, take Rt. 528 exit off I-90. Go south to Griswold. Turn left and continue to Emerson. Turn left and continue to Doty. Turn right on Doty and look for the winery on the right.

From Erie, take Rt. 534 off I-90. Go south to South River Road. Turn right and look for the winery on the right.

Chalet Debonné Vineyards…the name gives it away: this winery is a haven for anyone looking for a break from everyday experiences. Debonné is a place just far enough out of the way from the hubbub to be as relaxing as a trip to a real chalet – far, far away.

"We are an endpoint," co-owner Tony Debevc says proudly. People go to Debonné not because they're passing through, but because this is where they like to go. Offering live entertainment, an outdoor grill, a bed & breakfast, and seasonal events year-round, there is always a reason to make this winery your destination.

To make the winery a success today, the Debevc's have had to endure and overcome many hardships in their history. The tradition started in 1916 with Anton Debevc planting a vineyard and making his own wine. This expanded over the years until Anton's son, Tony Sr., and grandson Anthony created Chalet Debonné Vineyards and

Debonné is a complete destination, with a grill, bed & breakfast, and more wine than you can drink.

opened for business in 1976.

Today, Tony operates the modern facilities carrying with him the spirit of the past, while his wife, Beth, takes care of the retail side of the winery. Both have their work cut out for them, but with their friendly smiles they make it seem so easy.

The "Debonné Vineyards" varietal wines prove how successful this region's *vinifera* wines can be, while the "Chalet Debonné" house wines continue the tradition of blended native and hybrid grapes.

"We try to make this educational," says Tony of his winery. He does his best to help customers understand what goes into the wine-making process. Full tours are given regularly and include all aspects of the winery.

"We also encourage our people to get out," notes Debevc, who believes that you cannot understand wine or know how good yours is unless you're actively trying wine from other producers.

As for the home front, Chalet Debonné grows about 90 percent of all grapes used in their wines. With over 80 acres of vineyards all with-in two miles of the winery, Debonné is a massive grape producer. Still, it must buy some regional grapes to meet its needs.

The wines here are all very good. To get a feel for Debonné's ability, try a tasting tray of their wines so you can compare

*U*niquities:

- *Complete destination! B&B, grill, and wonderful wine.*
- *Famous for their many festivals.*

varieties and styles. Then, pick a place to enjoy your bounty, either inside in the bar or grill area, out front on the porch, or on the wine-glass-shaped patio out back.

If the weather suits, you may not want to leave! The scenery from either outside location is outstanding. You can sit there as long as you'd like; the Debevc's are more than happy to have you!

Debonné is known for its many popular festivals. Annual events include an Easter Egg Hunt, Family Fun Day, Candlelight Cellar Tastings, Hot Air Balloon Rally, and the nuttiest one of all: Crazy Hat Day. Whatever day you pick to visit Chalet Debonné will be a great one, just don't plan leaving any time soon.

Wine Selections:

Pinot Gris: Very fresh, floral and crisp. Great example of this wine!
Country Selections White: Semi-dry blend of *vinifera* & hybrid grapes.

Debonné's Sweet Apple Relish Pork Roast

Ingredients:
3 lb boneless pork roast
1 cup sauerkraut (chopped cabbage may be substituted)
1 onion, chopped
1/2 cup Riesling wine
1 jar sweet pepper & apple relish
your favorite seasonings

Preheat oven to 325. Place pork roast in roasting pan, cover, and bake for 2 hours. After 2 hours, pour the remaining ingredients over the roast and place back in the oven for at least one hour. (Time may vary for larger roast.)

This is a fantastic dish served with red skin potatoes.

Serve with Chalet Debonné Harmony.

(This recipe was submitted by the staff of Chalet Debonné.)

CLAIRE'S
GRAND RIVER WINERY

Founded:	1977
Owners:	Al and Joanne Schneider
Winemaker:	Bill Turgeon
Address:	5750 South Madison Road
	Madison, OH 44057
Phone:	(440) 298-9838
Hours:	Sunday, Wednesday, Thursday 1 p.m. to 7 p.m.
	Friday and Saturday 1 p.m. to 1 a.m.
Annual production:	N/A
Price range of wines:	Starting at $8.50 US
Amenities available:	Indoor and outdoor seating, tours and buses welcome, restrooms.

Directions:

Take the Rt. 528 exit off I-90 and go south. Continue for three miles and look for the winery on the right.

Just three miles south of I-90 on South Madison Road sits Claire's Grand River Winery. Hidden down a long driveway behind thick, green foliage is a winery with a powerful mission.

While the winery has been around for many years, it's recently under new ownership. Joanne and Bill Schneider purchased the winery for a number of reasons. One stands out from the pack.

"We bought it to feed a foundation," says Joanne, as she spells out Claire's Grand River Winery's role as a funding source for "Faith Foundation," a charity founded to assist poor and middle-class people who find themselves in financial difficulty.

"We try to help them and keep them from falling through the

General Manager Greg Henderson, making sure everything's in place at Claire's Grand River Winery.

cracks," Joanne explains.

The Schneiders have also purchased Old Mill Winery in Geneva and a gift shop and a coffee house all to feed the foundation. While they both work full-time jobs, they've hired Greg Henderson as general manager to run the winery day-to-day.

"This is the best job I've ever had in my life," says Greg, as he explains how he supports the cause with his heart and soul. With extensive night club and restaurant experience, Greg fits right in.

"Joanne started out with nothing," he says, illustrating how far the foundation has come.

Claire's Grand River's wine is created by winemaker Bill Turgeon, who also makes the wine for Old Mill. He uses the winery's 52-acre vineyard for most of his wine, while buying some juice from local sources.

While the wine may draw a lot of customers to Claire's Grand River Winery, it's the entertainment that brings the bulk of business. Dueling pianos ring in every Friday and Saturday night, bringing in lots of people, that ultimately helps the foundation.

Uniquities:

- *Profits from winery feed a charity foundation in Cleveland.*
- *Dueling pianos every Friday & Saturday night.*

"The whole purpose is to make money to give to the foundation," Greg says. He is excited to be a part of the Schneider's vision, and hopes to see many new faces grace the winery in the future.

While there's no Claire on the payroll, she's definitely hard at work at the winery. "Claire" means pure, holy – much reminiscent of the winery itself.

Make a stop at Claire's Grand River Winery to enjoy fine wine, great entertainment, and food, all while helping the Faith Foundation of Cleveland grow. As Greg says, "It's all good things rolled into one."

Pan Seared, Coriander Dusted Sea Scallops with a Golden Beet, Chive Vinaigrette

Ingredients: (As is, this makes 10 portions.)
18-20 oz scallops
1 cup golden beets
1/2 cup raspberry vinaigrette
1 1/2 fluid oz olive oil
1/2 cup chicken stock
2 tbsp chives, chopped
salt, to taste
white pepper, to taste
coriander, crushed, to taste

In a non-stick pan, sauté the scallops until golden brown. Cook the beets in their skins until they are fork tender. Puree the beets while slowly adding the raspberry vinaigrette, olive oil and chicken stock. Add salt and white pepper to taste.

(This recipe was submitted by Brandt Evans, executive chef at Kosta's restaurant in Cleveland, Ohio.)

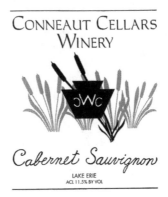

CONNEAUT CELLARS WINERY

Founded:	1982
Owner:	Joal Wolf
Winemaker:	Joal Wolf
Address:	P.O.Box 5075, (Rt 322 & Rt. 6)
	Conneaut Lake, PA 16316
Phone:	(814) 382-3999, (877) CCW-WINE
WWW/E-mail:	www.ccw-wine.com
Hours:	10 a.m. to 6 p.m., 7 days a week
Annual production:	7,200 cases
Price range of wines:	$5.95 - $18.95 US
Amenities available:	Wheelchair accessible, gift shop, restrooms, picnic area.

Directions:
Take exit 36-B off I-79. Proceed six miles west on Rt. 322 to Conneaut Lake. The winery is on the left, just across from the lake.

When Joal Wolf purchased Conneaut Wine Cellars in 1996, it came with a tradition of well-respected wine from a well-respected family: his own. Shortly after his father's death, Joal decided to buy the winery from his mother to continue the family's wine tradition.

This was not Joal's first foray into wine, though. He'd been the assistant winemaker at Conneaut under his father's direction for many years. While learning the craft, he attended Pennsylvania State University to earn a master's degree. Soon after, he became winemaster under the watchful eye of his father.

"We're not out to impress anyone," expresses Joal. His boisterously friendly personality, combined with his down-to-earth approach to wine, immediately makes everyone at home.

Wolf grows no grapes of his own. He buys them from local grow-

At Conneaut Cellars Winery, you'll experience interesting conversation and good wine.

ers, feeling that he has more quality control by purchasing the best of the best in the region. This distinctive fruit has helped him win both national and international awards over the years.

The wines at Conneaut Cellars vary in styles ranging from very dry, barrel-fermented Chardonnay, all the way to Hazel Park Red, a sweet, creamy-tasting wine named for Hazel Park, located just on the east side of Conneaut Lake. At first, the proprietary names of most of the wines can be overwhelming. But, once you begin tasting the care that has gone into each and every wine, you'll be at ease.

"We want people to say 'this is a must-see stop,'" Joal says. If it isn't already, it should be: Joal offers a wide variety of gifts to go along with Conneaut Cellars' assorted wines. To help narrow the choice of wines to taste, Joal has given each wine a number from 0-4 to gauge sweetness, and with up to twenty wines available at a time, this is a great help!

"We don't pretend to make French or California wine," says Joal, protesting the idea that all wine should fit a mold. His wines are uniquely crafted in a style unto their own.

Take a tour of the facilities while visiting the winery and you'll notice some fresh paint: Joal is always planning the next expansion while finishing up the current round. "A lot of money gets put into this winery to do what we do well."

Uniquities:

- *Situated right on Conneaut Lake, Pennsylvania's largest inland lake.*
- *Wonderful wines named after local lore.*

But in the end it's not the winery's expansion or success that matters to wine lovers, it's the wine. As Joal says, going to Conneaut Cellars is like going to grandmother's house – "you get the real good home feel and taste."

Wine Selections:

Chardonnay: Oak-fermented sur-lie style, this very dry wine smells of apples and vanilla.

Allegheny Gold: Semi-sweet white made from Vignoles. Warm apple aromas make this a winner.

Pymatuning Rose: This semi-sweet rosé is citrusy and balanced, made from *labrusca* grapes.

Sadsbury Red: Old oak barrels aged this semi-dry Chancellor wine.

Hazel Park Holiday Cake

Ingredients:
1 box Duncan Hines yellow cake mix
1 3-1/2 oz French vanilla instant pudding mix

3/4 tsp ground nutmeg
1/3 cup vegetable oil
4 large eggs
1 cup Hazel Park Cream Red Wine

Grease a 9-10 inch tube cake pan, preheating oven to 350.

Mix all ingredients with a mixer on low speed until all ingredients are moist. Then beat on high speed for 2 minutes. Stop mixer and scrape bowl then beat on high for 1 additional minute. Pour batter into prepared tube pan and bake in preheated 350 oven for about 50 minutes. Test cake for doneness.

Cool for 25 minutes, then loosen from bottom and sides of tube pan and continue to cool on a rack. Remove from tube pan when completely cool. Sprinkle with confectioner's sugar if desired.

To make a less rich cake, omit oil and pudding mix, reduce eggs to 2 eggs and increase the wine to 1 1/3 cups.

Serve with Hazel Park Cream Red Wine.

(This recipe was submitted by Joal Wolf of Conneaut Cellars Winery.)

AMERICAN
CHARDONNAY
Barrel Fermented

MADE AND BOTTLED BY FERRANTE WINE FARM, INC.
HARPERSFIELD TOWNSHIP, GENEVA, OHIO
ALCOHOL 11% BY VOLUME

FERRANTE
WINERY & RISTORANTE

Founded:	1937
Owners:	The Ferrante Family
Winemakers:	Nicholas Ferrante; Anthony Ferrante, Sean Bogart, cellarmasters
Address:	5585 State Route 307 Harpersfield Township Geneva, OH 44041
Phone:	(440) 466-VINO (8466)
Hours:	Monday - Tuesday 10 p.m. to 5 p.m. (Wine Sales Only!) Wednesday - Thursday 12 p.m. to 8 p.m. Friday - Saturday 12 p.m. to 10 p.m. Sunday 1 p.m. to 6 p.m.
Annual production:	38,500 cases
Price range of wines:	$5.99 - $14.99 US
Amenities available:	Wheelchair accessible, gift shop, restaurant, outdoor seating, restroom.

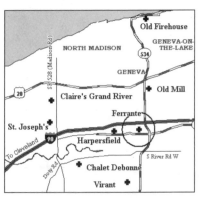

Directions:

Take the Rt 534 exit off I-90 and go south to Rt. 307. Turn right and the winery will be on your right.

It's no surprise that the Ferrantes make fine wine: their secret is years of experience and their Italian-ness. Ok, so while the Italian part does play an important role, it's the decades of winemaking experience that really pay off.

Wine and Ferrantes have gone together since 1937, when Anna and Nicholas Ferrante started their family's winemaking tradition. They started the tradition in Cleveland's Collinwood area, bringing in grapes from their Geneva vineyards. This lasted until 1979, when Peter and Anthony Ferrante brought the winery to the much more scenic vineyards in Geneva's Harpersfield Township.

In the early '80s, the inevitable happened: the Ferrante family opened a full-service Italian restaurant to alleviate the hunger of guests for years to come. This other family tradition has been a pop-

Ferrante's pavilion overlooking the vineyards is complemented by a fountain.

ular attraction at the winery, as it's a fusion of two favorite past-times of winery-goers.

In November 1994, the restaurant was ravaged by a fire, but fortunately the winery and cellars were spared. With the rebuilding of the restaurant to greater grandeur in 1995, the current incarnation of the Ferrante Winery and Ristorante was born.

The new building houses offices, the restaurant, gift shop, and tasting area. It is bright and feels very spacious due to the huge windows that line the walls. High ceilings, a fireplace and outside seating for winetasting and light fare make this more than just a functional space – it's artistic and fun.

The wines are a melting pot of styles and varieties, meaning there should be something for all tastes at Ferrante. Whether it's the jammy Cabernet Franc or the bright and fruity White Catawba, winemaker Nicholas Ferrante puts maximum effort into his wines' quality.

Nicholas hints at some sparkling wines in the near future, and with their new fully-automated bottling line and pristine facilities, expansion is not an issue. Growing enough grapes, on the other hand, can make or break these grandiose ideas.

"We're planting new vineyards to keep up," says Nicholas. The Ferrantes' 36 acres are quickly expanding to include more Chardonnay, Cabernet Franc and Vidal. Keeping up with their own winemaking needs is almost as challenging as staying ahead of the public's demand for their wine!

*U*niquities:

- *Wonderful restaurant with a diverse menu of entrees.*
- *Quickly expanding with a greater variety of wines every year.*

There are three things you should keep in mind when visiting Ferrante Winery and Ristorante: wine, food and gifts. You'll walk out of the winery well fed, well wined, and – if you take advantage of their expansive gift shop – well gifted, too.

Call ahead to get a schedule of events at the winery. On any given day, you can experience great live music on the outside terrace, other wonderful events, or you can just enjoy the beautiful landscape and listen to the birds and fountain competing for your attention.

Wine Selections:

Rosso: Clean, semi-sweet pasta red. Perfect with rich, red sauces.

ecipe

Ferrante Ristorante's Veal Vidal

Ingredients:
4-5 oz primo veal slices
8 oz sliced mushrooms
1 tsp minced garlic
2 cups Ferrante Vidal Blanc Wine
1 cup Karo white syrup
4 oz butter
4 tbsp olive oil
1/4 cup flour
salt/pepper to taste

Heat olive oil in saute pan. Flour veal and place in hot oil. Saute veal. Add mushrooms, garlic, salt & pepper. Brown veal evenly on each side. Remove pan from heat and deglaze with Ferrante Vidal Blanc wine. Add Karo syrup and butter. Reduce sauce until thickened. Serve with side of pasta and vegetable of your choice. Serves 4.

Serve with Ferrante Vidal Blanc.

(This recipe was submitted by the Ferrante Family.)

HARPERSFIELD VINEYARD

Founded:	1986
Owners:	Wes Gerlosky & partners
Winemakers:	Wes Gerlosky
Address:	6387 Route 307
	Geneva, OH 44041
Phone:	(440) 466-4739
Hours:	Wednesday - Thursday 12 p.m. to 8 p.m.
	Friday - Saturday 12 p.m. to 10 p.m.
Annual production:	3,000 cases
Price range of wines:	$12.00 to $30.00 US
Amenities available:	Light fare served, restrooms, outdoor seating, wheelchair accessible.

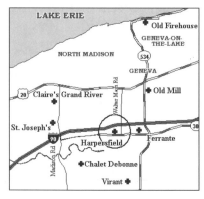

Directions:

From Cleveland, take the Rt. 528 exit off I-90. Take Rt 528 south to Rt 307. Turn left and continue for four miles. Winery will be on the left.

From Erie, the Rt. 534 exit off I-90. Take Rt 534 south to Rt 307. Turn right and continue for about four miles. Winery will be on the right.

"Small is beautiful," chimes Wes Gerlosky, while giving a tour of his winery. Indeed. Harpersfield produces only 3,000 cases of wine a year, but this is enough to spread his cheer to his critiquing customers. Gerlosky is a fine winemaker, believing that a wine's balance is everything. This belief has done nothing but great things for his wines.

He's an easy man to believe. Gerlosky is a tall, stately figure who towers over most of his customers, commanding instant respect from all who meet him. Instantly likable, he is warm and friendly; attesting to this are the many returning customers whom he knows by name.

You may notice some unfamiliar wines on Harpersfield's wine list. Don't worry: they're all of utmost quality. Auxerrois and Kerner, while not familiar varieties in the United States, are used to make fine wines in Germany. "A lot of odd-ball vines make really excellent wines," Gerlosky says as he tastes his Kerner. His Chambourcin

Harpersfield's bounteous tasting room awaits your visit.

has vivid blackberry aromas and a spicy, peppery flavor. Expect totally balanced wines here.

The tasting room at Harpersfield is a fairly recent, but welcome, addition to the winery. Inside, you'll find fine, wine-related art, dried flowers hung around the room, a large banquet table and many small tables at which to relax and enjoy the surroundings. And the fresh bread. And the gourmet cheeses. The bread is baked in a stone, wood-burning oven and is served by the baguette or with cheese and fresh fruit – a perfect complement to Harpersfield's wines.

Gerlosky is both admired and feared among other Lake Erie vintners. He is known for his expert winemaking techniques, as well as his sharp tongue when it comes to quality. "Quality is so incredibly fragmented in the region," Gerlosky says. "Some guys' vision is only as far as their nose – they taste only their wine and never gain perspective."

While his critiques of the region's wines as a whole may sound harsh, his soapbox – his wine – is sturdy. He points out that the Lake Erie region's wines are going in the right direction.

Truly one of the region's most masterful winemakers, Gerlosky is not the least bit pretentious when it comes to talking about his wines: he tells you how and why he made them that way. Open to questions, he's always willing to dish out advice to attentive ears.

_U_niquities:

•_Some of the region's best wines._
•_Unusual varieties of wine._
•_Fresh bread from stone,_
wood-burning oven -
right in the tasting room!

When visiting Harpersfield, allow some time to enjoy the accommodations. If you have time, call ahead to find out if there are any special tastings scheduled. At these tastings, Gerlosky "brings people up to speed on world wines," by offering many different wines one region at a time. Live, learn, and drink superb wines at Harpersfield.

Wine Selections:

Kerner: Interesting Muscat flavors; possibly only Kerner in U.S.
Chardonnays: All of them are exquisite! A few different styles.
Gewürztraminer: Alsacian style, with flavors of spice and lychee nut.
Chambourcin: Old-vine wine. Blackberry aromas, smooth finish.

Potato & Leeks in Phyllo

Ingredients:
2.5 lbs Idaho potatoes
1 bunch leeks
1/2 lb chevre goat cheese
salt, pepper, garlic to taste

1 lb butter
1/2 lb bacon
1 package phyllo dough
Olive oil

Peel and quarter potatoes and boil as you would for mashed potatoes, cooking until slightly tender in the meantime

Melt the butter and set aside
Clean and dice leeks in a hot skillet. Saute leeks until they begin to turn brown (caramelize). Set them aside, cook off bacon. When done, roughly chop.

Set aside remembering to also save the grease when potatoes are cooked. Drain and put back into the pot. Add caramelized leeks, bacon, bacon grease, chevre, garlic, salt & pepper to taste.

On a clean, dry counter top, lay out one sheet of defrosted phyllo dough, lengthwise. Brush entire sheet with butter. Repeat until you have a layer of 4 sheets.

Take potato leek mixture and spread a layer along the bottom edge of the dough (mixture should start at edge of pastry and work in toward center until about 1/2 inch in height).

Gently fold outside edges of dough over the leek mixture.

Fold over a second time and roll until you have what resembles a cylinder, pinch shut the edges. You will have what looks like a Tootsie Roll. Brush with butter and lay on a slightly oiled sheet pan.

Repeat until potato mixture is gone. Bake them in 375 oven for about 20 minutes or until golden brown. Remove from oven and let set about 5 minutes. Cut into bite-size slivers for aperitif or in longer sections and use as a side dish.

(This recipe was submitted by Harpersfield Vineyard.)

AMERICAN
RIESLING

JOHN CHRIST
WINERY

Founded:	1946
Owner:	Bob Forlini
Winemakers:	Andy Andro, Mac McLelland, assistant
Address:	32421 Walker Road
	Avon Lake, OH 44012
Phone:	(440) 933-9672
Hours:	Monday - Thursday 10 a.m. to 6 p.m.
	Friday - Saturday 10 a.m. until midnight.
Annual production:	6,300 cases
Price range of wines:	$3.07 - $9.46 US
Amenities available:	Wheelchair accessible, restrooms,
	hospitality room.

Directions:
Take Rt. 83 exit off I-90 and go north to Walker Road. Turn right on Walker and follow to the winery on your right.

John Christ Winery has been around for a very long time. Since its creation by Macedonian natives John and Toda Christ in 1946, the winery has undergone some expansive changes.

For one thing, the production has grown. It now produces over 5,000 cases of wine per year. The ownership has changed as well, and the new owners are putting a greater emphasis on making *vinifera* wines.

"One of my present goals is to make quality *vinifera* wines," says Mac McLelland, assistant winemaker. The wine list has expanded to include Cabernet Sauvignon, Merlot, Chardonnay and Riesling – all while complementing the high-quality *labrusca* and hybrid wines that John Christ has made for decades.

The inclusive wine list is a strong point for John Christ Winery. Having *vinifera*, *labrusca* and hybrid wines available can only increase sales and visits to the winery. All three varieties are made exceptionally well.

John Christ's back porch overlooks the vineyards – perfect for a relaxing glass of wine.

Some fruit wines have been added to balance out the list. Christ's blackberry, peach and raspberry wines have all won awards, and they will probably win yours, too.

It's usually hard to find a respectable Cabernet Sauvignon for under $10, but John Christ Winery has succeeded in producing a rich and toasty wine that rates well in both the taste and price categories.

The rest of the prices are great, too. For just $4.49, you can get an award-winning "Special Blend" wine – a "half & half" with Niagara and Concord.

John Christ currently grows 25 acres of Concord, Niagara and a few hybrids and buys most of their *vinifera* from neighboring growers.

A few years back, the previous owners built a hospitality room to the back of the winery. With a wine bar and room for a band, its popularity has grown over the years.

"It's a big part of our business," says Mac. A wonderful supplement to wine sales, the hospitality room has become a draw in and of itself. If warm enough to leave the wood-stove heated room, check out the lovely deck overlooking the vineyards. With tables and chairs at which to relax and sip wine, the back porch is a great place to end a long day.

*U*niquities:

- *Hospitality room is open late on weekends and is a great place to just sit and talk.*
- *Nice mix of old and new varieties of wines.*

If you're planning ahead, call to get the dates of the winery's summer and fall events. The steak cookout, perch fry and clam bake are each worth a visit!

Wine Selections:

Chardonnay: A "summer Chardonnay," says Mac. Light and fruity.
Special Blend: Real sweet and real good; half Niagara, half Concord.
Peach: Top-of-the-line on the sweetness scale and real, real peachy.

Brandt's Sturgeon with Plum Tomato, Caper & Dill Butter Sauce

Ingredients:
7 oz white california sturgeon - center cut fillet

Sauce:
4 oz shallots
8 oz white wine
3 oz lemon juice
1 tbsp tomato paste
1 1/2 lb unsalted butter, softened
1 cups plum tomatoes
2 tbsp capers
2 tbsp dill - fresh, chopped

Combine the shallots, wine, and lemon juice and reduce until there's no moisture left in the pan. Gradually whisk in the butter over medium heat. When emulsified, add plum tomatoes, capers and dill. Sauté sturgeon in a pan with clarified butter or oil until golden brown. Finish in 400 degree oven for 5 minutes. Put on plate and top with sauce.

Serve with John Christ Chardonnay.

(This recipe was submitted by Brandt Evans, executive chef at Kosta's restaurant in Cleveland, Ohio.)

33050 Webber Road
Avon Lake, Ohio 44012
LAKE ERIE

VIDAL BLANC
A German-style White Varietal

KLINGSHIRN
WINERY

Founded:	1935
Owners:	Allan & Barbara, Lee & Nancy Klingshirn
Winemaker:	Lee Klingshirn
Address:	33050 Webber Road
	Avon Lake, OH 44012
Phone:	(440) 933-6666
Hours:	10 a.m. to 6 p.m. daily.
	Closed Sundays and holidays.
Annual production:	4,600 cases
Price range of wines:	$3.99 - $16.99 US
Amenities available:	Wheelchair accessible, restroom.

Directions:
Take Rt. 83 exit off I-90 and go north to Webber Road. Turn left on Webber and follow to the winery on your right.

After passing through a typical residential neighborhood on Webber Street, the road narrows and the winery gradually appears to the right. While the building looks fairly modern, the history inside stretches back to the days of prohibition.

During the chill of prohibition, Albert Klingshirn operated a business selling grape juice to area home winemakers. Shortly after repeal in 1935, he opened his own family farm winery – all in the cellar of his home.

Expansion was quick, and soon Albert had a bustling two-level winery adjacent to his home. In 1955, Albert's son, Allan, bought the winery and vineyard land and began planting hybrid grapes to replace some of the native grapes his father had grown.

By 1978, the winery was four times its original size! Lee Klingshirn, Allan's youngest son, grew quickly into the family busi-

Watch for humming birds when entering the winery: they constantly flutter around the vine-covered walls.

ness. He studied Viticulture and Enology at Ohio State University and upon graduation eased his way into the title of "winemaker."

Lee is continuing the family's tradition by planting more and more *vinifera* grapes in the vineyard. Although he feels European varieties like Riesling are perfect for the region, he acknowledges his customers' love for the American varieties. This won't stop him, though.

"I think our Riesling is as good as any in the world," asserts Lee. Taste and find out.

Klingshirn's twenty wines cover the palate. From dry Cabernet Sauvignon to Sweet Concord to White Riesling Champagne, Lee offers wines for all tastes. Lee claims his wines are lighter, more delicate, and fruitier. In the tasting room, you'll also find gifts, touring brochures, and…Karma.

"Karma, is our vineyard protection," says Lee, as he pats his dog on the back. Karma acts as security enforcement in the vineyard, defending it from crows, deer and grape-loving raccoons.

"The buck stops here," claims Lee, who is the only full-time employee at the winery. His parents, Allan and Barbara, work regularly, but Lee is held responsible for most of the winery's activity.

A bit of a naturalist, Lee notes how much wildlife is present in the area, especially in his vineyard. "Vineyards are real good for bird life," says Lee, who always sees bluebirds and other species when working outside. You don't have to look to the vineyards to glimpse some flighty friends, though, as humming birds circle around the front door, trying to get to the flowering vines that cover the winery's walls.

*U*niquities:

- *Long family tradition of winemaking.*
- *Some very good, innexpensive wines, including a variety of sparkling wines.*

Klingshirn's small tasting room ensures one-on-one service. Bottles of wine await sale along every wall. Some, at just $3.99 a bottle, are gone shortly after bottling. As long as there's this strong demand, Lee promises to make more. He's got a long family tradition to uphold, and he'll definitely keep his word!

Wine Selections:

White Riesling: Semi-dry, balanced with honey and apricot aromas.
Contemporary Blend Champagne: Unique Seyval and Vidal blend.

Klingshirn Grape Chiffon Pie

Use one 9" baked pie shell

Filling:
2/3 cup sugar
1 package unflavored gelatin
1 1/2 cups grape juice
3 egg yolks
1 1/2 tbsp lemon juice

Mix ingredients together in saucepan. Cook over low heat stirring constantly until mixture boils.

Boil for 1 minute. Remove from heat and chill until slightly thick.

Meringue:
3 egg whites
1/3 tbsp cream of tartar
6 tbsp sugar

On high speed, beat egg whites until soft peaks form. Slowly add the cream of tartar and sugar, continue to beat until mixture is stiff.

Fold meringue into chilled grape filling. Pour gently into pie shell.

Chill until firm. Top with whipped cream before serving.

(This recipe was submitted by Lee Klinghirn of Klingshirn Winery.)

Since 1968

Markko

Reflections
of Lake Erie

Chardonnay

Grown, Produced and Bottled By
Markko Vineyard, Conneaut, Ohio
Alcohol 11 % by Volume

MARKKO VINEYARD

Founded:	1968
Owners:	Arnie Esterer and Tim Hubbard
Winemaker:	Arnie Esterer
Address:	4500 South Ridge Road
	Conneaut, OH 44030
Phone:	(440) 593-3197, (800) 252-3197
WWW/E-mail:	www.markko.com, markko@suite224.net
Hours:	Monday - Saturday 11 a.m. to 6 p.m.
	Closed Sunday.
Annual production:	2,100 cases
Price range of wines:	$7.50 - $30.00 US
Amenities available:	Wheelchair accessible, restroom.

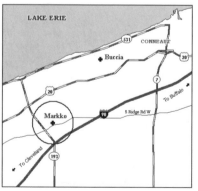

Directions:
Take Rt. 193 exit (exit 235) off I-90 and go north to blinking light. Turn right on Main St. As the road slopes down and curves right, it becomes South Ridge Road. The road turns to gravel and the winery is on the right.

Nestled in the forest just south of I-90, Markko Vineyard has a reputation among fine-wine drinkers for producing consistently excellent *vinifera* wine. If this is what you crave, seek and ye shall find your prize at the dwelling of winemaker Arnie Esterer.

Esterer glows with an inner tranquility, and this is most definitely transferred to his wines.

This peace may stem from his association with the Benedictine order, in which he is an Oblate, or friend of the Benedictines.

Esterer was inspired to grow *vinifera* grapes by the legendary Dr. Konstantin Frank, Finger Lakes wine-maker and propagator of the notion that most everyone can grow European *vinifera* grapes. This idea was radical to most winemakers in the region, who thought the climate was too cold to support these more deli-cate grape varieties.

"I heard what he was doing and had to meet him," says Esterer, who says he was astonished to

Arnie, Linda and their bearded friends await your arrival!

hear of Dr. Frank's success. When Esterer arrived on his doorstep, the imposing Dr. Frank asked, "Who are you? A somebody or a nobody?"

"I'm nobody," replied Esterer, trembling, hoping to have spoken the right answer.

"Good. Let's go to work," grumbled Dr. Frank.

From that encounter on, Esterer has been a firm believer that to make wine of utmost quality, you must use *vinifera* grapes. His beliefs have made a world of difference. The wine you taste at Markko is unparalleled by all but a few in the region.

Esterer chose this land with the winery in mind, and his 14 acres of vineyards are thriving as a result of the careful planning.

Linda Frisbee, vineyard manager since 1976, is attuned to every vine and tends to them with the end result in mind. All grapes are grown on-site, which puts great responsibility on Frisbee through-out the growing season.

Her efforts are realized in Markko's wine. Not one, but up to five Chardonnays grace Markko's wine list, with Riesling, Cabernet Sauvignon and Pinot Noir also standing strong.

Esterer creates most of his wine for the long haul, claiming that their higher acid allow for years of aging. Some get more intense over the years, while others sim-ply evolve into a smoother state of being.

A second label, "Covered Bridge," offers lighter styles of Riesling, Chardonnay and Picnic Red, each retailing for $7.50.

*U*niquities:

- *Outstanding Chardonnays, Rieslings and Cabernets.*
- *Very quiet location, set off the road amidst a forest of tall trees.*

Markko's tasting room is quaint and rustic, with the focus of the space being a large table at which guests can relax and prepare. Here you will be treated to Esterer's insightful conversation and his deeply introspective wines.

All of Esterer's wines are exquisite, and a visit is mandatory if you enjoy serious, European-style wines. Follow the gravel driveway to the winery on the right, and don't be alarmed when the gray-beard-ed welcoming party greets you. Arnie, with his four-legged partners, Matilda, Willie and their offspring will gladly guide you to some of the finest wine east of the Rockies.

Wine Selection:

"Homage" Chardonnay: Ripe fruit and rich oak flavors, smooth.

Sautéed Chliean Sea Bass with a Spicy Asian Red Bell Pepper Coulis

Ingredients: (As is, makes 10 servings)
10 6-oz portions of Chilean sea bass
12-14 red rell peppers, or 6 lbs
1 tbsp garlic
1 tbsp shallots
1 cup white wine
1/2 cup sugar
3 oz pickled ginger
1 tbsp red pepper flakes
4 oz oyster sauce
1 qt chicken stock
2 oz olive oil

In a non-stick pan, sauté the bass until it is golden brown then finish in the oven until the desired internal temperature is reached.

Coulis
Rough cut the bell peppers, shallots, and garlic. Sweat these until tender. Add wine, stock, and sugar. Reduce the mixture until there's no remaining moisture in the pan. Remove and puree in a food processor/blender. If the coulis becomes too thick, add water. Finish coulis by adding diced pickled ginger, oyster sauce and red pepper flakes.

Serve with Markko's Dry Riesling and/or Reflections of Lake Erie Chardonnay.

(This recipe was submitted by Brandt Evans, executive chef at Kosta's restaurant in Cleveland, Ohio.)

OLD FIREHOUSE
WINERY

Founded:	1988
Owners:	Old Firehouse Partners
Winemakers:	Don Woodward
Address:	5499 Lake Road
	Geneva-on-the-Lake, OH 44041
Phone:	(440) 466-9300, (800) UNCORK-1
Hours:	Late June-Labor Day: Every day 12 p.m. to 1 a.m.
	Labor Day-Dec 31:
	Monday - Thursday 12 p.m. to 7 p.m.,
	Friday - Saturday 12 p.m. to 12 a.m.,
	Sunday 1 p.m. to 5 p.m.
	January 1 - mid April: Fri-Sat 12 p.m. to 11 p.m.,
	Sun 12 p.m. to 5 p.m.
Annual production:	6,300 cases
Price range of wines:	$5.99 - $13.50 US
Amenities available:	Wheelchair accessible, restaurant, restrooms.

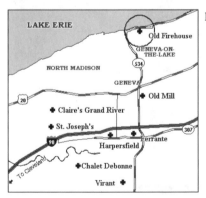

Directions:

Take Rt. 534 exit off I-90 and follow north through Geneva-on-the-Lake. When the road becomes Rt. 531, the winery will be on your left. If you pass the waterslides, you've gone too far.

As you pull in to Old Firehouse Winery's parking lot, you'll notice two things. First, there's "Old Betsy," a pristine 1924 Graham Brothers fire truck marking your destination. Then, just to the left and straight back, is Lake Erie. Old Firehouse Winery is lakefront property at its finest.

If this sounds perfect, imagine bringing the kids and not having to worry about them while you taste wine and enjoy the scenery. It's as easy as sending them to the adjoining amusement park and you're hassle-free for the day.

Don Woodward, winemaker and part owner of the winery and amusement park, can be seen walking around in a blue shirt and red suspenders. He's a third-generation volunteer firefighter, and all-around fire truck fan. This is a hidden passion only until you enter the tasting room. Look up, and you'll see hundreds of fire trucks and other firefighting paraphernalia arranged on the overhead beams.

"Old Betsy," who once served her community, now guards Old Firehouse Winery.

But before you sample the wine, it's worth considering whether or not you're going to take advantage of the winery's full restaurant, the Firehouse Grill. There you can order light fare items, or go for an entire meal ranging from traditional American cuisine (burgers and lake perch) to full Mexican dinners.

The restaurant has seating indoors, out back on the patio, or up on the deck, which overlooks the lake and the amusement park.

"Grandpa made awful wine," says Woodward. "I still couldn't

drink it!" Woodward grew up in a firefighting, winemaking family. His grandfather inspired him to make good wine, and also to become a volunteer firefighter in Geneva-on-the-Lake. "He stayed on the local firehouse's active roster until he was 98 years old," says Woodward, attesting to his grandfather's persistence and spirit.

Woodward's wine is a work in progress. "We're always trying new things and improving," Woodward says as he reviews his wine list. Old Firehouse offers 20 wines in all styles. From cherry, spiced apple, and red raspberry to Firehouse Red and Johannisberg Riesling, Woodward provides tastes for every palate.

Recently added to the lineup is the Spumante Champagne, a semi-sweet sparkler that breaks away in character from the rest of Old Firehouse's wines. This rounds out an already impressive list of wines suitable for beginning wine lovers and the artfully skilled alike.

Uniquities:

- *Winery is in Geneva-on-the-Lake's original fire house.*
- *Full restaurant with outside deck and view of Lake Erie.*
- *Amusement park next door!*

Make a point to wander down to the lakefront to take in the beautiful view. Woodward is planning a lakefront deck in the near future. Until then, you'll have to imagine yourself enjoying a bottle of wine on the deck with the lake lapping the shore beneath your feet, and maybe, just maybe you'll block out the cheerful screams of the kids on the waterslide in the park next door!

Wine Selections:

Lighthouse Niagara: This sweet white makes a great sipping wine.

Seyval Blanc: Dry and medium-bodied with a tart finish.

Country Cabernet: A combination of Ruby Cabernet and Cabernet Franc make this a full-bodied and zesty wine.

Woody's Wine-y Pudding

Ingredients:
4 egg yolks
2 tbsp of powdered sugar (fine cane sugar suggested)
3 tbsp of Old Firehouse Red or other sweet to semi-sweet wine

In a double-boilder, bring the water below to HOT, but do NOT let it boil.

Add the yolks and sugar, beating constantly using a high quality French whip.

While beating, and when JUST starting to stiffen, slowly mix in the wine. Keep beating until mixture begins to hold its shape, but is still smooth. Pile immediately into heated thick cups if you are going to serve warm. Be careful not to scrape sides of boiler. If you have overheated the mixture, the crust on the bowl will ruin the texture. If the mixture separates, you have either overheated it or over-whipped it.

An alternative is to serve VERY cold. Then you would put into custard or sherbet cups and chill.

"My favorite is warm," says Woody. "When chilled, the flavor of the wine is masked and it is just another boring pudding type dessert!"

Serve with simple wafers.

(This recipe was submitted by Old Firehouse Winery's Don "Woody" Woodward.)

OLD MILL WINERY

Founded:	1980
Owners:	Al and Joanne Schneider
Winemaker:	Bill Turgeon
Address:	403 South Broadway
	Geneva, OH 44041
Phone:	(440) 466-5560
WWW:	www.oldmillwinery.com
Hours:	Sunday, Tuesday - Thursday 1 p.m. to 9 p.m.
	(6 p.m. during winter),
	Friday - Saturday 1 p.m. to 1 a.m.
Annual production:	N/A
Price range of wines:	Starting at $8.50 US
Amenities available:	Bar, wheelchair accessible, restrooms.

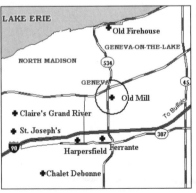

Directions:
Take Rt. 534 exit off I-90. Go north over one set of railroad tracks and look for red winery building immediately on the right.

Old Mill Winery's painted red building once thrived as a grist mill. When it was bought and converted to a winery in 1980, new life was breathed into it, and it has become a warm gathering spot for locals and tourists alike.

When you walk inside, a saloon-type atmosphere surrounds you. If you're not wearing your boots, don't fret – this winery is for everyone! Old Mill is so much more than just a haven for wine lovers. It has a large bar and lots of tables for relaxing and eating a light meal prepared by the staff at Old Mill. Enjoy the live entertainment booked on most weekends throughout the year.

History lines the walls of the main room in the form of newspaper articles and photos, and on the back wall of the building you can look at artifacts from the grist mill's high time.

Behind the bar stands Keith Childers, Old Mill's general manag-

Old Mill Winery is a nice place to try some new wines and see some of the area's history.

er. This friendly, quiet guy is easy to get along with and will guide you through a tasting of Old Mill's diverse wine list.

Make yourself at home, and order something from the "Munchie Menu" as you verse yourself in Old Mill wine.

Old Mill Winery is owned by Joanne and Al Schneider, owners of Claire's Grand River Winery. Both wineries are used to raise funds for the Faith Foundation of Cleveland, a charity dedicated to helping the poor and middle-class people in financially difficult times.

"We bought both to take 50 percent of the profits to feed the foundation," says Joanne. Old Mill has grandly aided in the Schneider's endeavor. Filled to the brim on Friday and Saturday nights, the winery provides a great evening of entertainment, complemented by good wine and food.

Some of Old Mill's wine is made at Claire's Grand River Winery where winemaker Bill Turgeon works his magic.

"Bill makes excellent, excellent wine," says Joanne, who had better be a fan! She is, and she truly feels that her wineries' wines are divine.

She's not the only one who feels that way. Both wineries have received ecclesiastical approbations from the Cleveland and Youngstown Dioceses granting them permission to make altar wine.

Uniquities:

- _Approved to make altar wine for Cleveland and Youngstown dioceses._
- _Winery is an old grist mill._
- _Some profits used for charity._

"This is the first time ever in local history," says Joanne, with pride and honor in her voice.

Old Mill Winery is steeped in tradition, and it's through a tour that you will come to know the great history of the winery and the former grist mill. Take a tour, enjoy one of their famous "wine burgers" and sample some wine – all while feeding a good cause.

Wine Selections:

Geneva Blush: Very similar to a White Zin. Light and fruity, made from _labrusca_.

Grindstone White (Cream Niagara): Wow! Sweet and popular.

Cabernet Franc: Very dry, with some depth and varietal character.

Recipe

Brandt's Smoked Salmon Tower

Ingredients:
6 oz smoked salmon
3 tsp red onion, finely diced
2 tsp capers
2 tbsp lemon zest
2 tsp fresh dill
1 ea. cucumber, sliced
1 tsp tobiko caviar
dill sprigs

Place a mold on a plate. Place cucumbers in the bottom and around the sides of the mold, overlapping each one over the previous. Take half of the smoked salmon and place in bottom of mold. Combine onions, capers, zest, and dill and place on top of salmon. Place remaining salmon on top. Finish off with a dollop of caviar. Garnish with sprig of dill.

Serve with Old Mill's Chardonnay.

(This recipe was submitted by Brandt Evans, executive chef at Kosta's restaurant in Cleveland, Ohio.)

ST. JOSEPH VINEYARD

Founded:	1997
Owners:	Art and Doreen Pietrzyk
Winemakers:	Art Pietrzyk
Address:	6060 Madison Road
	Thompson, OH 44086
Phone:	(440) 298-3709
Hours:	By appointment only.
Annual production:	1,200 cases
Price range of wines:	$9.00 - $25.00 US

Directions:
Take the Rt. 528 exit off I-90 and go south. Continue for a few minutes and the winery will be on your right.

While St. Joseph Vineyard may be one of the newest commercial wineries in the region, owners Art and Doreen Pietrzyk are not neophytes to the vine.

"We've been growing *vinifera* grapes at this location for 13 years," says Art as he shows guests around his immaculate vineyard. These six to seven acres are where the Pietrzyks grow every grape they use to make their wine.

"By growing our own grapes, we have total control of the quality and characteristics we want," Art says. He has one of the few locations in the region that can support Pinot Noir, a notoriously finicky vine. Art and Doreen pluck leaves around every cluster of grapes to ensure perfect sun-ripening.

Art is an engineer, and this is immediately apparent once you taste the intricate detail to which he has refined his wines. With roughly eight wines available, guests can explore the fine art created

Joseph Pietrzyk walks from St. Joseph Vineyard's winery and tasting room.

at this small winery.

"To achieve our style and quality of wine here in Ohio, we have to hand-craft everything and limit production like Porsche," says Art as he pours a glass of his tremendous Pinot Noir Reserve. These aspirations are not far from being met. The Pietrzyks' wines are all excellent, but the Pinot and Riesling stand apart from most in the region with their intensity of fruit and genuinely balanced bodies.

St. Joseph's tasting room sits directly above the wine cellar, but you'd never know it. The winery building is just behind the owners' home and pole barn. In fact, guests park in their driveway right in front of their garage. It's a small, but attractive one-room building with a big, sliding-glass door marking the entrance. The tasting room is rustic and sometimes takes on the feel of a wilderness cabin.

When Art needs to get another bottle of wine for tasting, he pops open a small trap door in the tasting room's hardwood floor and shimmies down into the cellar (around back, there's a utility entrance that doesn't require a climb).

Art and Doreen have no plans to outgrow their status as a boutique winery. They plan to add some wines to their list in the near future, including Sauvignon Blanc, Pinot Blanc, Merlot and an Ice Wine. Follow their progress through the years, and enjoy their new creations.

Uniquities:

- *Amazing Pinot Noir, all made from estate grapes!*
- *Small winery built directly above cellar.*
- *Open by appointment only.*

The winery's name and colorful stained-glass logo and label impart a religious feel. The name, though, was inspired by Joseph, Art and Doreen's son. The St. Joseph Winery's brochure says that "You will know them by their fruits" (Matthew 7:16), and you will.

"Wine-growing is our avocation," says Art, his eyes glimmering with enthusiasm. This is so obvious once you meet the Pietrzyks, taste their wines, and understand the warmth and passion apparent in both.

Wine Selections:

Chardonnay: Slight citrus and tropical flavors. Very full and oaky.
Riesling: Superb example. Semi-dry with melon and citrus flavors.
Pinot Noir: Luscious strawberry fruit and smokey tones. Very light.

Medallions of Pork

Ingredients:
1 1/2 lbs pork tenderloin, cut into 3/4" thick slices
1/4 cup coffee cream
dry bread crumbs (seasoned)
2 1/2 tbsp butter or margarine
salt and pepper to taste
1/4 cup finely chopped onions
1 1/2 cups sliced mushrooms
1/2 cup Riesling
parmesan cheese
1/2 cup coffee cream

Dip pork slices in 1/4 cup cream; then coat with bread crumbs. Wrap in wax paper and chill one hour to set bread crumbs. Melt 1 1/2 tbsp butter in skillet and brown pork. Remove to shallow baking pan.

Season with salt and pepper. Saute onion and mushrooms in same skillet, adding last tbls butter. Cook a minute or two while stirring. Spoon mixture on top of meat.

Drizzle wine over all and sprinkle with Parmesan cheese. Cover with alumnium foil and bake at 350 degrees for 20 minutes. Uncover and pour cream around edges; continue baking, uncovered 5-10 minutes longer. Makes 4 servings.

Serve with St. Joseph Reisling and red potatoes.

(This recipe was submitted by Art & Doreen Pietrzyk of St. Joseph Vineyard.)

MADE AND BOTTLED BY
VIRANT FAMILY WINERY, INC.
1250 STOLTZ ROAD
GENEVA, OHIO 44041.

Red
Velvet
(MEDIUM SWEET)

RED VELVET IS A MEDIUM
SWEET RED WINE, AND HAS
A VINEYARD FRESH AROMA
& GRAPE FLAVOR WITH A
SMOOTH FINISH.

RED TABLE WINE

LAKE ERIE

ALCOHOL 10% BY VOLUME

VIRANT
FAMILY WINERY

Founded:	1998
Owners:	Charlie, Martha, Frank and Holly Virant
Winemaker:	Charlie and Frank Virant
Address:	1250 Stoltz Road
	Geneva, OH 44041
Phone:	(440) 466-1314
Hours:	Monday - Friday 2 p.m. to 6 p.m.
	Saturday 12 p.m. to 6 p.m.
	Sunday 1 p.m. to 5 p.m.
Annual production:	630 cases
Price range of wines:	$7.00 for all wines (or $15.90/gallon) US
Amenities available:	Wheelchair accessible, restroom.

Directions:

Take the Rt. 528 exit off I-90 and go south. Turn left on Cork Cold Springs Road. Turn right on Stoltz and the winer will be on your left.

"They're the only grapes we know," says Charlie Virant as he settles comfortably into his chair. He's talking about native American *labrusca* grapes, and Virant has made them its specialty.

Charlie's grandfather and father made wine, and he's been making it for over 30 years, so surely he knows what he's doing, right? "It's not just pick 'em and squeeze 'em," he says, laughing at how most people think winemaking is an easy trade.

"We make a pretty fair wine," Charlie says humbly. He and his son Frank are in charge of winemaking, while Martha and daughter-in-law Holly control the retail half of the operation.

Charlie says he and Martha love to chat with their guests. "If they want to talk, we'll talk!"

Charlie described how a customer once stopped by late at night to get wine for a family gathering the following day. Never mind the hour, Charlie opened the winery and made the sale. "We'll open for

The Virant Family Winery is the mecca of quiet Stoltz Road, with cars coming and going regularly.

anyone," he said with a youthful smile.

"People like to come here because it's quiet," adds Martha, who says people come to Virant to "get away." The winery consists of 17 acres of grapes, a small winery building with a tasting room, and the driveway leading up to it. "We're small and we make wine the old fashioned way," says Charlie. They'll give tours and show you how they make their tempting wine, but they won't give away all their secrets.

Charlie says they often taste wine brought by customers. "They bring their home wine for us to comment on – there's a lot of great wine out there," he says.

The Virants enjoy having people over. Lots of people. Their summer event schedule alone typically has 10 major events listed. Food and featured bands create a lively atmosphere that turn this quiet farm into an instant party. Pig beef roasts, pasta dinners, clambakes and chicken dinners…It's obvious they love food. So do their customers.

"We have good food, and people know it," Charlie says without hesitation.

People know the wine, too, and Virant is quickly gaining a loyal following of fans. Since opening in March of 1998, Virant Family Winery has grown steadily, mostly through word of mouth. They hope you too will spread the word once you try their very traditional "American" wines.

*U*niquities:

- *Produce labrusca wine only!*
- *Complete family operation: Charlie, Martha, Frank or Holly will greet you upon arrival.*

The family dogs may greet you when you arrive. Have no fear, because they're as friendly as the Virants, and the most they'll do is show you to the winery's entrance. Once inside, one of the Virants will tend to all your wine-tasting needs.

Wine Selections:

Red Satin: A sweet and traditional Concord.
White Lace: This dry wine shows an unusual side of Niagara.
White Silk: Sweeter, more traditional Niagara.
Pink Delight: Very full, fruity Catawba.

Recipe

Martha Virant's Homemade Grape Pie

Ingredients:
4 cups concord grapes
1 cup sugar
3 tbsp flour

Remove skins from grapes and set them aside. In saucepan, heat pulp of grapes without water, just to boiling and while it's hot, rub through strainer to remove the seeds.

Mix strained pulp and skins together. Stir sugar and flour together and mix with grape mixture.

The ingredients for the crust are:
2 cups flour
1 tsp salt
3/4 cup Crisco
1/4 cup water

Bake for one hour at 350 degrees.

Serve with Virant Red Satin.

(The first recipe was submitted by Martha Virant of Virant Family Winery.)

Regional Suggestions

Restaurants:

Biscotti's
186 Park Avenue
Conneaut, OH 44030
(440) 593-6766

Sandalini's Bistro
18228 Conneaut Lake Road
Meadville, PA 16335
(814) 724-1286

The Clay Street Inn
2092 State Route 45
Austinburg, OH 44010
(440) 275-5151

Season's Grille
1752 South Broadway
Geneva, OH 44041
(440) 466-4638

Kosta's
2179 W 11th St
Cleveland, OH 44113
(216) 622-0011

Silver Shores
Rt 322 & US 6
Conneaut Lake, PA 16316
(814) 382-4471

Lou's Billow Beach
5205 Lake Road West
Ashtabula, OH 44004
(440) 964-7930

Tony's/Golden Anchor
1001 Harbor St
Conneaut OH 44030
(440) 599-8669

Accommodations:

Buccia B&B
518 Gore Road
Conneaut, OH 44030
*(On the vineyard estate
of Buccia Vineyard)*
(440) 593-5976

The Grapevine B&B
6790 South River Road
Geneva, OH 44041
*(On the vineyard estate of
Chalet Debonné Winery)*
(440) 466-7300

Lakehouse Inn B&B
5653 Lake Road
Geneva-on-the-Lake, OH 44041
(440) 466-8668

Liberty Inn
353 Liberty St.
Conneaut, OH 44030
(440) 599-9767

Polly Harper Inn
663 N. Stoltz Road
Geneva, OH 44041
(440) 466-6183

Local Attractions:

Ashtabula County offers tons of historical & educational sites & tours.
(800) 337-6746 • www.accvb.org

Cleveland waterfront and various museums
(too much to list! Pick up a complete tour guide when in the area)

Conneaut Historical Railroad Museum
363 Depot St. • Conneaut, OH 44030 • (440) 599-7878

Covered bridges galore in Ashtabula County

Pymatuning Lake offers camping, fishing, swimming and boating.
(724) 927-9358

Western & U.S. Islands Region

No poem was ever written
by a drinker of water.

— Homer

Lake Erie's Western
& U.S. Islands Regions

Sandusky and Port Clinton, Ohio, are the last stops on the mainland before heading off to the islands. Firelands Winery is a great first stop, as it's the "mother" winery of Mon Ami and Lonz wineries. There you can find information to plan your island adventures and get a taste of what's being produced using grapes grown on the islands.

In the past, Ohio's islands were some of the best known grapegrowing regions in the country. The original Kelley's Island Winery started planting in 1850. According to Kirt Zettler, of Kelley's Island Wine Co., by 1860 land on the island was going for $2,000 an acre! By 1900, 26 wineries had settled on the island – there was not a tree in sight due to the expansive vineyard plantings.

Nowadays, wineries are few and far between on the islands, but the winemaking tradition is still vivid in the minds and the glasses of island wine lovers.

For the typical land-dweller, your first moments on the islands produce priceless expressions. There is such vibrant life on the

islands during the summer, and it's impossible to count all the bicycles and golf carts adorning the streets. Cars are common, but golf carts and bicycles rule as the primary means of transportation around the islands.

If you are planning a day trip to the islands, it is not necessary to bring

In Put-in-Bay, golf carts rule the road – easy to rent, easy to park! your car. The added expense is not worth the hassle, as bikes and carts are cheap to rent and easier to park.

The U.S. island wineries – Heineman, Lion Hill, Kelley's Island Wine Co., and Lonz – all produce good wine, but it is not so much the wine as the atmosphere that makes the excursion valuable.

When I first docked in Put-in-Bay, I was struck with the vacationland atmosphere all around. Music blaring, people celebrating any- and everything imaginable, and activity – nonstop activity – bustling as far as the eye could see.

Some considerations while planning a trip to the island wineries:
1. Check the weather to make sure your departure and arrival times will be storm-free. When bad weather picks up, it does so quickly and with a vengeance.

2. Double-check ferry schedules and note that each one leaves from a different location, so don't get stuck waiting in line for the wrong ferry.

3. If you'd like to visit more than one island winery (most likely on different islands), check to see which ferry goes to each, or which one goes to all. It may save you time and money.

4. Dress according to the weather report, but always bring backup. And remember, you can't just run back to the car to get your jacket when you're stranded on an island in the middle of Lake Erie!

A note on Pelee Island Winery and Wine Pavilion:
Pelee Island Winery, located in Kingsville, Ontario, Canada, also has a Wine Pavilion on Pelee Island, where it offers winetasting, tours, concerts and other activities. Since the winery itself is located in Ontario, I've put it in the "Lake Erie's Northern Region" section of the book, where it's described in detail. Plus, the island is a lot closer to mainland Canada, so traveling from Pelee Island Winery in Kingsville would be a better option than from Ohio.

FIRELANDS WINERY

Founded:	1980
Owners:	Paramount Distillers
Winemaker:	Claudio Salvador
Address:	917 Bardshar Road
	Sandusky, OH 44870
Phone:	(419) 625-5474, (800) 548-WINE
WWW/E-mail:	www.firelandswinery.com
Hours:	June-Sept: Monday - Saturday 9 a.m. to 5 p.m., Sunday 1 p.m. to 5 p.m.
	Oct-Dec: Monday - Saturday 9 a.m. to 5 p.m.
	Jan-May: Monday - Friday 9 a.m. to 5 p.m., Saturday 10 a.m. to 4 p.m.
Annual production:	600,000 gallon capacity
Price range of wines:	$5.90 - $11.70 US
Amenities available:	Wheelchair accessible, restrooms.

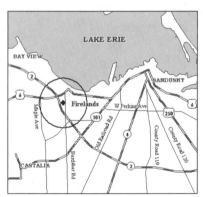

Directions:
Take Rt. 2 to the Rt. 6 exit. Turn east to Bardshar Road, then turn right and follow to Firelands Winery on your right.

You don't have to ask many people about Ohio's North Coast wineries before becoming very familiar with Firelands' name. This is the second largest winery in the state, with a capacity of 600,000 gallons of wine. Long before you turn into the winery's parking lot, you'll see the three tremendous tanks signaling your arrival.

Firelands' is owned by Paramount Distillers, a conglomerate that also owns three other well-known regional wineries: Lonz and Mon Ami and Ohio's largest winery, Meiers.

Claudio Salvador is winemaker for and vice-president of Firelands. He has on his plate a huge chunk of responsibility making wines for these three premier wineries. He came to America

Firelands is your gateway to Lake Erie's western and island winegrowing regions.

after earning an enology degree in Italy. He and Ed Boas, Firelands' president, both entered the Firelands family in 1984. Since then, they have expanded production of *vinifera* varieties.

The winery began in 1880 as Mantey Winery, named after owner Edward Mantey, a German immigrant. He bought 35 acres, built his winery, and began a long tradition making fine eastern varietals like Concord, Catawba and Niagara. The Mantey family sold the winery to the Firelands group in 1980, but is remembered on every bottle of Mantey wine that Firelands continues to produce today.

Firelands now produces wine under four labels: Firelands, Mantey, Mon Ami and Lonz.

Firelands' Pinot Grigio is rich and elegant while the Pinot Noir has subtle flavors and a long finish. Their sparkling wines are all made in the classic French "methode champenoise" style but their Riesling Champagne is the most unique, retaining some typical Riesling characteristics while exuding perfect bubbles.

Boas feels Firelands excels at some of the Alsacian varieties like Pinot Grigio and Gewürztraminer. Their *vinifera* wines are all made in classic styles and will be much appreciated by lovers of European wine styles.

"We know we're good, but it's nice to have our peers recognize us," says Boas, referring to Firelands' Gewürztraminer, which was recently awarded a Double Gold medal and "Best of Class" in the San Diego International Wine Competition.

Uniquities:

- *Huge production capacity and expansive facilities.*
- *Educational winery tour.*
- *Makes wine for Mon Ami and Lonz wineries, too.*

If you're interested in a great winery tour, Firelands is the perfect place to start. With an extended multi-media presentation and tour of the facilities along an elevated walkway, Firelands gives its customers a truly inside look into day-to-day operations.

"It's one of the better technical tours given in the region," says Boas, who is very interested in educating his customers about the winemaking process.

The care put into this operation is apparent when you try any of Firelands' wines. Claudio Salvador tends to each one individually, ensuring that each glass of Firelands wine is of utmost quality.

Wine Selections:

Walleye White: A blend of white wines, very balanced and smooth.
Cabernet Sauvignon: Mildly tannic and complex due to its oak aging.

Firelands COQ Au VIN

Ingredients:

-8 ounces unsmoked bacon, thickly sliced
    and cut into matchstick-size pieces
-3 tbsp unsalted butter and 3 tbsp peanut oil
-2 broiling chickens, each cut into 2 breast
    halves, 2 legs, 2 thighs, and 2 wings
-flour for dredging
-1/4 cup Paramount Brandy
-pinches of salt & freshly ground black pepper
-12 boiling onions, peeled with a cross cut
    into the root end
-1 additional tbsp of unsalted butter
-1 large shallot, minced
-1 clove garlic, minced
-2 cups Fireland's Cabernet Sauvignon
-1 cup rich unsalted veal stock, or canned
    low-sodium beef broth

-2 tbsp tomato paste
-a *bouquet garni* consisting of 1 bay leaf,
    2 parsley sprigs, 3 sprigs fresh thyme
    (or 1 tsp dried leaf thyme), and
    2 cloves; tied in dampened cheesecloth
-8 thin slices high quality bread, cut into large
    triangles or discs, brushed with butter
-8 ounces small button mushrooms, whole,
    or if the mushrooms are large, quartered
    or thickly sliced
-1 additional tbsp unsalted butter
-1 additional garlic clove, peeled & crushed
-a slurry of 2 tbsp potato starch and 3 tbsp
    water or Cabernet Sauvignon
-salt & freshly ground black pepper, to taste
-minced fresh parsley, for garnish

Crisply fry the bacon pieces in a mixture of butter & oil. Remove them from fat & reserve them on a paper towel.

Very lightly flour the chicken pieces & brown them. Then, carefully, flame the chicken pieces in the brandy. Reserve chicken pieces on a plate. Very lightly salt & pepper them.

Add the boiling onions to the pan, browning them lightly. Remove onions & reserve. Pour all of the browning fat out of the pan. Replace with a tablespoon of butter. Lightly sauté the shallot & garlic, taking care not to let them burn.

Add Firelands Cabernet Sauvignon & veal stock or beef broth to the pan, scraping any coagulants from the pan's bottom inside & incorporating them into the sauce. Stir in tomato paste. Add *bouquet garni*.

Return the chicken, bacon lardoons, & onions to the sauce. Cover & gently simmer for 30 minutes over medium low heat…or bake in preheated 350-degree oven. (This can also be done easily in an electric skillet.)

While the chicken is cooking, lightly sauté some bread croutons in clarified butter. Reserve in a warm place. Also, lightly sauté the mushrooms in a tiny amount of butter seasoned with a tiny piece of peeled & crushed garlic (discard the garlic after sautéing). After 30 minutes, add the mushrooms to the chicken & simmer an additional five minutes.

After a total of 35 minutes, remove the chicken pieces, mushrooms, & onions to a warm platter. Garnish with croutons & reserve, lightly covered with foil.

Over high heat, reduce the sauce by 50%. Thicken with the slurry to a desired density. Adjust seasoning with salt & pepper, to taste. Allow to cook & additional five minutes, then spoon over the chicken pieces. Sprinkle with minced parsley. Serve at once.

(This recipe was submitted by Tom Johnson, Corporate Chef, Paramount Distillers, Inc.)

HEINEMAN WINERY

Founded:	1888
Owners:	Ed and Louis Heineman
Winemaker:	Ed Heineman
Address:	978 Catawba St.
	Put-in-Bay, OH 43456
Phone:	(419) 285-2811
WWW:	www.ohiowine.com
Hours:	April-Nov 15th: Mon-Sat 10 a.m. to 10 p.m.
	Sun 12 p.m. to 7 p.m.
Annual production:	13,000 cases
Price range of wines:	$6.50 - $10.55 US
Amenities available:	Wheelchair accessible, restrooms, light-fare menu, picnic area.

Directions:

Take ferry to Put-in-Bay, South Bass Island. Follow Catawba St. to the winery on your left.

When you arrive at Heineman's, watch out for the tram that shuttles hundreds of visitors to and from the winery each day. Just a short bike or golf cart ride from the heart of Put-in-Bay, the winery makes for a wonderful family visit.

While you're at the winery, it's a must to take a guided tour of Crystal Cave, the largest known geode in the world. The walls are covered with crystals and the tour takes you down through the cave, which is about 30 feet in diameter. A combined tour of the cave and winery is available from early May until late September. With the nominal admission charge, you receive a glass of wine (or grape juice!) and great commentary about both attractions.

Once on site, you'll probably run into Louis Heineman, grandson of founder Gustav Heineman. Louis is outgoing and friendly, and he hardly acts his age. He is the "master of the house," supervising operations at the winery, continually checking in with the tasting room's staff and his son Ed, Heineman's chief winemaker.

Heineman is a busy place throughout the summer, with island trams bringing hundreds of customers daily.

All is usually well, as this winery has survived even the harshest of all trials: prohibition.

When prohibition became a reality, Louis' father, Norman Heineman, kept the business alive by selling grape juice to home winemakers, who by law could produce 200 gallons of their own wine for personal use. Norman, winemaker at Heineman until 1950, promoted this by including winemaking instructions with every juice sale. The winery survived through the era of these

oppressive laws, and immediately started thriving again when prohibition was repealed.

Louis started making wine in 1950 and remained winemaker
until Ed graduated from Ohio State in 1980. He's still in charge of
the wine and is continually trying new things. He's even considering adding a Merlot to the list in the future.

The wine list has just about everything on it – native *labrusca* wines
like Concord and
Niagara, hybrids like
Vidal Blanc, and
vinifera like Chardonnay
and Riesling. "Our
bread and butter are our
sweet wines," Ed Heineman
says.

"Wine is all a matter
of individual taste," says
Louis, explaining why
they offer so many
wines. He says they
offer something to
make each customer
happy. It's tough keeping

*U*niquities:

- *Founded in 1888!*
- *Biggest attraction in Put-in-Bay.*
- *Tour the winery and Crystal Cave, 2 for 1 deal.*

up with the changing tastes of his customers. Even Louis' tastes have
changed over the years. "Wine is like salad dressing: sometimes you
want oil and vinegar, sometimes you don't."

Heineman is probably the most popular attraction on the island.
And the family heritage continues with Ed, and now with his son
Dustin. Still too young to drink, or even work at the winery, Dustin
helps out after school and during the summer, when they need all
the help they can get. He's got a good thing to inherit in the form
of Heineman Winery.

Wine Selections:

Island Blush: Triple award-winner. Semi-dry and very fresh.
Burgundy: Blend of Concord and Ives, making a light, semi-dry red.
Pink Catawba: Heineman's #1 seller. No wonder!

Mrs. Pollak's Baked Walleye

Ingredients:
3-4 lbs walleye
1 tbsp flour
1/2 tsp sugar
1 onion, chopped fine
1/2 cup Parmesan cheese
1/2 cup bread crumbs
1 1/2 cups sour cream
butter
horseradish

Bake walleye at 400 degrees.

Saute the onion chopped fine, in butter until light brown. You can do this in a microwave – onions don't burn. Then, mix with 1 1/2 cups sour cream, sugar and flour. Mix all ingredients together and spoon over fish for 10 minutes at 400 degrees again.

Cut up fish (take a 9x12 inch pan) and cut in 2 inch squares. Grease pan with butter. Lay fish in pan and dot with butter. Bake at 400 degrees for 10 more minutes.

Put ingredients over fish and bake at 400 degrees.

Take Parmesan cheese and bread crumbs, mix real well and sprinkle over fish and bake till light brown at 400 degrees for 10 minutes. Take horseradish with tablespoon and put around the sides of pan.

Serve with Heineman Island Chablis.

(This recipe was submitted by Myrtle M. Pollak, Put-in-Bay, Ohio.)

ALCOHOLIC CONTENT 12% BY VOLUME

LAKE ERIE
HAUT SAUTERNE
PRODUCED AND BOTTLED BY
JOHLIN CENTURY WINERY
OHIO BONDED WINERY NO. 69
OREGON, OHIO 43616
Contains Sulfites

JOHLIN CENTURY WINERY

Founded:	1870
Owner:	Rich Johlin
Winemaker:	Rich Johlin, Jarrod and Bolan Muchewicz
Address:	3935 Corduroy Road
	Oregon, OH 43616
Phone:	(419) 693-6288
Hours:	Monday - Saturday 11 a.m. to 6 p.m.
Annual production:	2,000 cases
Price range of wines:	$4.40 - $7.00 US

Directions:

From the East, take Rt. 2 west past Port Clinton. Turn right on Wynn Road and follow to Corduroy Rd. Turn left on Corduroy Rd. and follow to winery on the right.

From Detroit and Toledo, take I-280 south/east to Front St. Turn left on Front St. and right on Consaul which becomes Corduroy. Winery is on your left.

When you arrive in Oregon, Ohio, there's not much to see or do. The area is part suburban, part rural, with Toledo being *the* big city around. A stop at Johlin Century Winery is a real treat, especially if you're on the way somewhere or just want to take a nice drive.

Take the brick driveway to the small parking lot next to the winery, take a look around you. A couple barns, a tall windmill tower and a large bell greet you.

The house right next to the winery is a focal point worth investigating. Built in 1870, it has housed the Johlin family for over 125 years. It adds such depth to the property it's no wonder why the Johlins stayed right where they were.

Once to the winery, a cheerily smiling Rich Johlin welcomes you. He's been the lone stranger at this winery for many years, but now he's really got something to smile about.

His two grandsons, Jarrod and Bolan Muchewicz, have joined the

Johlin's brick drivways and paths guide you to the heart of their operation.

Johlin Century Winery team and are giving Rich a hand. As fifth-generation winemakers at Johlin, they have a lot of pride and success to carry into the next century.

While the Johlins' farm is no longer in full production, they used to raise just about everything on the land. "Beans, cattle – you name it," says Rich. Now that Rich has help, he'll surely be taking a break from years of working alone. Luckily, his grandsons are ecstatic to have joined the Johlin team.

The only change Johlin's wines have seen over the years are some new tanks. The wines are made in the traditional old American style: nice and easy.

You can taste Johlin's wines in the quaint tasting area. What could have been a hallway has been converted into the tasting room, with information on the left and shelves stacked with wine on the right.

All of the wines are processed in stainless steel tanks and bottled with screw caps.

There's a sign in the tasting area that sums up the humor and good nature of these guys. "If you are grouchy, irritable, or just plain mean, there will b e a $10 charge for putting up with you," it reads. This $10 may be worth it if you like sweet grape and other fruit wines. A visit to Johlin Century Winery is an experience you'll remember.

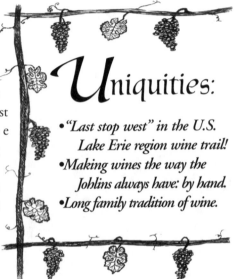

*U*niquities:

- *"Last stop west" in the U.S. Lake Erie region wine trail!*
- *Making wines the way the Johlins always have: by hand.*
- *Long family tradition of wine.*

When in the area, you may want to explore Maumee Bay State Park, just five minutes from Johlin. It's a popular vacation spot offering camping, swimming, boating and a lodge located right on Lake Erie. Beyond that, visit Toledo and explore the riverfront shops, or try the COSI museum located in the heart of the city.

Wine Selections:

Creme Niagara: Smooth and fruity; a local favorite.
Blackberry: One of two in the region. "Just like grandma's." says Rich.
Vin Rose: Very nice, semi-sweet and tasty.

Brandt's Berry Napoleon Dessert

Ingredients:
4 ea. Phyllo dough sheets
2 cup heavy whipping cream
4 tbsp powdered sugar
2 tbsp frozen raspberry syrup
1 cup melted butter
1 tbsp vanilla extract
fresh berries (seasonal)

Lay out each individual phyllo sheet and brush them with melted butter. Cut the sheets into 4" x 4" squares, place them on a baking sheet and bake them at 375 for about 8 minutes or until golden brown.

In a mixing bowl, begin whipping the cream. When the consistency begins to change, add the powdered sugar and continue whipping until a hard peak is reached. Fold in the raspberry syrup, vanilla extract and fresh berries. Create a tower by alternating layers of phyllo squares and the berry mixture.

Serve with one of Johlin's sweet fruit wines (author's suggestion: Johlin Blackberry).

(This recipe was submitted by Brandt Evans, executive chef at Kosta's restaurant in Cleveland, Ohio.)

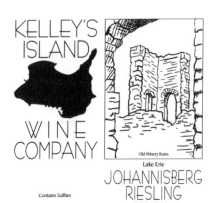

KELLEY'S ISLAND

WINE COMPANY

Old Winery Ruins
Lake Erie
JOHANNISBERG
RIESLING
Alcohol 11% By Volume

Contains Sulfites

KELLEY'S ISLAND
WINE COMPANY

Founded:	1981
Owners:	Kirt and Robby Zettler
Winemaker:	Bill Brashear
Address:	418 Woodford Rd.
	Kelleys Island, OH 43438
Phone:	(419) 746-2678
Hours:	Open daily at 10 a.m.
Annual production:	2,300 cases
Price range of wines:	$8.25 - $12.25 US
Amenities available:	Wheelchair accessible, gift shop, restaurant, full
	bar, restrooms.

Directions:

Take Neuman Ferry or Kelleys Island Ferry to the island. Take Water St. to Division St. north, then take right on Chapel to Woodward. Follow to winery on right.

As with the other island wineries, getting *to* the island is an experience in itself. On a beautiful summer day, the boat or ferry ride to Kelley's Island is full of maritime pleasure. On the other hand, if you're trying to get to or from the island during a storm, or during the winter months, you're in for frustration or a thrill.

Once you make it to the island, you can easily make your way to Kelley's Island Wine Co. by bike, golf cart or car. As you pull into their driveway, you'll see immediately why this is the most popular destination on the island.

"Probably 80 percent of the people who come here are not regular wine drinkers," says Kirt Zettler, co-owner with his wife Robby, of Kelley's Island Wine Co. The winery is more than just that: it's a full-service restaurant, bar and all-around hang-out.

During the summer, you'll be greeted with butterflies waiting their turn on the Zettler's many butterfly bushes. Past the swarm you'll find the new building that houses the deli, gift shop and, of

Kelley's Island Wine Co.'s new building is a welcome sight to parched travelers.

course, the tasting room.

The tasting room is actually the bar of the restaurant that makes up Kelley's Island Wine Co.'s retail space. It's one big open room with tables at which to sit, relax and enjoy a meal with some wine, or you can shimmy up to the bar for an official winetasting. Clean and new, the facilities are welcoming. The black and white checkered floor adds a nice touch to an already attractive room.

Since the island is relatively isolated during winter, the Zettlers installed a pool table that becomes a primary form of cold-weather entertainment. The atmosphere is light and there's no question of the Zettlers' dedication to this establishment. You will notice something not many other wineries offer: beer.

"I'm not a wine snob," announces Kirt as he displays his imported beer and microbrew list for the restaurant. Sometimes wine is not always the answer, and for those times, Kirt has selected only the best beer for his customers.

The "Grilling Deck," as the Zettlers call it, is on the side porch of the winery's new, main building. They grill outside at least five times a week! Everything from ribs to portabella mushrooms to the catch of the day make their way from the grill to the menu on a regular basis.

*U*niquities:

- *New, bright restaurant and tasting room.*
- *Kelleys Island: great getaway!*
- *They grill food outside on deck FIVE times a week!*

Kirt Zettler and his parents started the winery in 1980, and Kirt and Robby recently bought them out, so a new generation's in charge now, and the changes are apparent.

Kelley's Island Wine Co. always offers between 6 and 8 wines for tasting. Winemaker Bill Brashear has been with the winery for six seasons. He spent 12 years as an amateur winemaker before entering the land of commercial winemaking.

He and the Zettlers are doing great things already, and Kelley's Island Wine Co.'s wine will only get better as the years go on.

Wine Selections:

Chardonnay: Nice and nutty, with a clean, dry aftertaste.
Glacial White: A crisp, semi-dry blend of Vidal and Cayuga.
Long Sweet Red: As Kirt says, "just like a paisano wine from Italy." Semi-sweet with a beautiful finish.

Robby's Walleye Chowder

Ingredients:
4 potatoes, sliced
3 onions, sliced
1 cup chopped celery
4 whole cloves
2 garlic cloves, crushed
2 tbsp fresh dill weed, chopped
2 lbs Lake Erie Walleye, cut into chunks
2 cups half-and-half
1/2 cup Kelley's Island Glacial White wine
1/4 cup butter
1 cup chicken broth
water/wine

In covered pot over medium heat, simmer onions, potatoes, celery, cloves, garlic, and dill weed in 1/2 cup water, 1/2 cup wine for 25 minutes or until vegetables are tender.

Add fish and remaining ingredients. Heat to boiling, reduce heat to low, cover and simmer for 10 minutes or until the fish flakes easily.

Serve with Kelley's Island Glacial White.

(This recipe was submitted by Robby Zettler of Kelley's Island Wine Co.)

LION HILL
WINES

Founded:	1998
Owners:	Leone DiCesare and Don Hill
Winemaker:	Leone DiCesare
Address:	229 Bay View Avenue
	Put-in-Bay, OH 43456
Phone:	(419) 285-5463
Annual production:	12,500 cases
Price range of wines:	$6.00 - $14.00 US
Amenities available:	Wheelchair accessible, restrooms, light-fare menu.

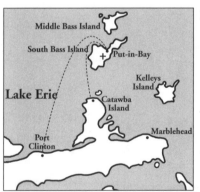

Directions:

From the main dock, follow to Bayview Avenue and he winery is on your immediate left before main park and Put-in-Bay city center.

This winery is the one exception in this book. While every other winery I've included uses grapes grown in the region, Lion Hill imports all its grapes from California. The reason for its inclusion? If you're already travelling to Put-in-Bay to visit Heineman's, it makes great sense to stop by Lion Hill for a taste of its award-winning wines.

Don Hill and winemaker Leone DiCesare wanted to make California and European style wines in Ohio, so in 1992 they created Lion Hill Wines. Lion Hill's main winery is in Warren, Ohio, but their main sales and tasting outlet, as well as limited production facilities, are at Put-in-Bay's Ladd Marina. Their shop offers wine-tasting, a full bar and a light-fare menu of snack and food options.

Specializing in Cabernet Sauvignon, Zinfindel, Barbera, Trebbiano, French Colombard and Chardonnay, Lion Hill wines are very respectable, but show none of the regional characteristics you'll find at the other wineries listed in this book.

All of the red wines are unfiltered and aged in oak barrels, and all

Decisions, decisions...Lion Hill's Put-in-Bay tasting room and bar offers wine, beer and mixed drinks.

wines are produced in small quantities. Winemaker Leone DiCesare has traveled the world developing his winemaking skills and has been recognized nationally for his talents.

"Totally different type of wine than what's made locally," says Don Hill, who is a full-time lawyer living on the island. Use this to your advantage and taste their wines to gain a perspective on what's being produced regionally. Stop by during summer nights for live entertainment, a light meal and some nice Ohio-made California wine.

LONZ
WINERY

Founded:	1884
Owners:	Paramount Distillers
Winemakers:	Claudio Salvador
Address:	Middle Bass Island, OH 43446
Phone:	(419) 285-5411
WWW:	www.firelandswinery.com/lonz
Hours:	May-Sept: Open daily from 12 p.m.
Annual production:	see Firelands Winery
Price range of wines:	$3.25 - 13.95 US
Amenities available:	Gift shop, snack bar, out-door seating, restrooms.

Directions:

Take a ferry to Put-in-Bay, South Bass Island, then hop the Sonny-S ferry or take Miller Boat Lines directly from the mainland to Lonz on Middle Bass Island.

With the winery commanding the every view of Lake Erie's Middle Bass Island, Lonz is hard to miss. This historic winery made its debut as the "Golden Eagle Winery" during the Civil War. By 1875, Golden Eagle Winery was the largest wine producer in the United States – not hard to imagine when you see how well grapes grow on the islands.

It was in 1884 that Peter Lonz became winemaker on the island, and his son George designed the castle-like building that has stood sturdy as the island's gateway for over a century.

Lonz has a tradition of hosting great entertainment throughout the summer. Combined with a gift shop and a snack bar serving

A view of the majestic Lonz Winery from aboard a ferry.

light meals, Lonz is a definite tourist destination. The gift shop sells Lonz wine, a variety of wine-related and nautical gifts, and some interesting art.

Today, Lonz Winery is simply a shell, importing all of its wine from the mainland where it's produced at Firelands Winery. Despite this, Lonz's wines, along with the building itself, are worth the trip to Middle Bass.

Most of the grapes used for Lonz's wines come from North Bass

Island, where limestone caves criss-cross the island allowing Lake Erie's water to warm the soil late into the season.

Lonz wines jump all boundaries to include everything from Lonzbrusco White to 3-Islands Madeira. Also available are a Spumante and the Ile de Fleurs Champagne, "Isle of Flowers" which is labeled with a replica of the hand-painted bottles of Lonz's past.

A tour of Lonz's cellars shows the winery's vaulted ceilings and deep, dark caves which stay naturally cool, protecting the wines during the hot summers. The huge oak barrels lining the walls are empty now, attesting to the transitional stage in which Lonz Winery currently stands.

Sadly, Lonz is up for sale. At press time, Lonz was still operating under the same owners. Hopefully its tradition will be maintained as a winery, but surely some good will come from the future ownership.

*U*niquities:

- *Was the largest winery in the country in the late 1800s.*
- *THE big attraction on Middle Bass Island.*
- *Castle-like, stately winery.*

Before venturing to Middle Bass, check the status of Lonz Winery. Make it a definite stop on your itinerary if it's still open – if for no other reason than the casual, yet medieval-castle like atmosphere.

Wine Selections:

Ile de Fleurs: Lonz's sparkler. Crisp, brut style.
3-Islands Ruby Port: Very nice, rich and velvety.
Sailor's Red: Dry red blend, full-bodied and low on tannins.

Broiled Pork Chops w/ Fresh Mushrooms & Spinach Braised in Port Wine

Ingredients:

2 loin pork chops, approximately 1 to 1 1/4-inch thick
Dry marinade consisting of: 1/4 tsp each - salt, pepper, crushed rosemary, ground clove, and minced fresh garlic
1 box frozen, chopped spinach, thawed
2 tbsp butter, or cooking oil
1 peeled shallot, or the whites of 2 scallions, finely minced
8 ounces fresh mushrooms, quartered
1/2 cup 3-Islands Ruby Port
2 tbsp heavy cream
salt, pepper, and grated nutmeg, to taste
1/2 cup shredded Swiss cheese or shredded skim milk mozzarella cheese

The day prior to serving, rub the pork chops with the dry marinade. Wrap them in plastic wrap and refrigerate. Twenty minutes before cooking, remove the chops from plastic wrap and wipe off any remaining dry marinade.

Preheat the broiler of a stove, setting the rack approximately 2 inches beneath the flame or coil, or heat a ridged stove-top broiler over medium high heat. Brush the ridges of the broiler pan, or stove-top grill with a tea-spoon of cooking oil. Broil the chops, approximately 5 minutes on each side. Remove to a warm place and cover with foil.

Concurrently, turn the thawed chopped spinach into a sieve and with a rubber spatula, press the excess water out of it. In a large, covered non-aluminum skillet, lightly sauté the shallot in the butter or oil, adding the mushrooms.

Cook for 5 minutes, then add the spinach, blending well. Add the beef broth and the 3-ISLANDS Ruby Port. Cover and braise over medium heat for 5 minutes. Uncover, raise heat to evaporate nearly all liquid. Then, stir in cream and season to taste with salt, pepper, and nutmeg.

To serve each chop, divide spinach and mushroom mixture between two oven-proof plates. Place a broiled chop on each bed of spinach. Sprinkle the cheese on top of each chop and spinach. Glaze under broiler and serve at once.

(This recipe was submitted by Tom Johnson, Corporate Chef, Paramount Distillers, Inc .)

MON AMI HISTORIC
RESTAURANT & WINERY

Founded:	1872
Owners:	Paramount Distillers
Winemaker:	Claudio Salvador
Address:	3845 East Wine Cellar Road
	Port Clinton, OH 43452
Phone:	(440) 797-4445
Hours:	Open year-round. Changes seasonally.
	Closed Monday and Tuesday off-season.
WWW/E-mail:	www.monamiwinery.com
Annual production:	see Firelands Winery
Price range of wines:	$4.80 - $13.80 US
Amenities available:	Wheelchair accessible, restrooms, full-service
	restaurant and banquet facilities.

Directions:

Take Rt. 2 to Rt.53. Go north on Rt. 53, crossing Rt. 163. Turn left on East Wine Cellar Rd. Winery is on your right.

Set beautifully on a hillside and surrounded by trees, the historic Mon Ami Restaurant and Historic Winery beckons to hungry wine lovers. The building is stately – built of stone with wood trimmings – but carries a warmth to it you cannot describe.

Built in 1872 as a winery, Mon Ami has huge vaulted ceilings in its cellar two stories below ground. The winery is no longer in use, and while the goods are produced at Firelands Winery, they retain the Mon Ami character that has made them famous.

"Mon Ami" means "you are my friend" in French. You get this feeling when dining in Mon Ami's extraordinary restaurant. The restaurant has garnered much respect over the years for its superb

Mon Ami's historic atmosphere creates great ambience when enjoying a meal, or just sampling wines.

meals that complement their award-winning wines. Whether you're dining in the formal dining area or the more casual Chalet, you'll discover the magic that makes Mon Ami so famous.

From stuffed mushrooms to escargot in garlic butter, ravioli fritta to New England style tenderloin tips, Mon Ami has more than enough exquisite options to tempt even the most finicky customer.

Mon Ami has been described as "the life of the region," due to the winery's year-round entertainment. Offering live outdoor jazz every Sunday from Memorial Day to Labor Day, Mon Ami could quickly become a regular hangout.

The wines also have a prestigious feel to them. You can sample them in the gift shop, try them by the glass at the bar, or by the bottle with a full meal in the restaurant. Mon Ami's brochure says, "Today, as yesterday, Mon Ami produces a full line of wines from Catawba to Cabernet Sauvignon." Although this is a spectrum of wine varieties, Mon Ami pulls it off eloquently.

At Mon Ami, the focus is not just on wine and food, but on the creation of these two most important aspects of each of our lives. Through the "Gilded Vine Cooking School," anyone can learn the basics – and intricacies – of cooking. Check Mon Ami's website for details about the program, or ask when you visit.

*U*niquities:
- *Great restaurant, wines and winery tour.*
- *Gilded Vine Cooking School, offered by chef Tom Johnson.*

A tour of the cellar illustrates the history that has made Mon Ami so special to so many generations of wine enthusiasts. Take a guided tour to learn the depth of Mon Ami's tradition and the promise in its future.

Throughout its operation, Mom Ami gives customers educational ways to better acquaint themselves with food and wine – the finer points of life.

Wine Selections:

Proprietor's Reserve Chardonnay: One of Mon Ami's premier wines. A bit of oak, with a smooth finish.

Cellarmaster's White: Blend of varieties with good fruit character.

Cabernet Sauvignon: Dark, round red with moderate tannins and full fruit flavors.

Bouillabaisse "Mon Ami"

Fish Broth

1 tbsp olive oil
1 large red onion, chopped
1 leek, white part only, sliced & rinsed
1 carrot, scraped & chopped
1 clove garlic, peeled & minced
2 cups diced tomatoes, seeded & juiced
1 potato, diced

1 tsp dried thyme
1 bay leaf
1 tbsp saffron threads, crushed
2 quarts fresh fish broth (above)
16 mussels, cleaned & bearded
1/2 lb uncooked shrimp, peeled & deveined
1/2 lb bay scallops, rinsed & trimmed

1 lb very fresh Lake Erie Walleye filet into 2" pieces
1 lb perch filets, each cut in thirds
salt & cayenne pepper, to taste
a splash of Paramount Anisette
a mixture of snipped Italian parsley and fresh basil
sauce Rouille (recipe follows)

Carefully wash fish bones, taking care to remove any bits of liver or intestines which may remain. Rinse chopped vegetables.

Combine all of these ingredients in a non-aluminum kettle. Bring to the boil. Reduce heat to a full simmer and cook, uncovered, an additional 20 minutes. Strain contents through a fine sieve into a clean bowl. Discard solids. Reserve broth.

The Soup

1 tbsp olive oil
1 large red onion, chopped
1 leek, white part only, sliced and rinsed
1 carrot, scraped and chopped
1 clove garlic, peeled and minced
2 cups diced tomatoes, seeded and juiced
1 potato, diced
1 tsp dried thyme
1 bay leaf
1 tbsp saffron threads, crushed
2 quarts fresh fish broth (above)

16 mussels, cleaned and bearded
1/2 lb uncooked shrimp, peeled and deveined
1/2 lb bay scallops, rinsed and trimmed
1 lb very fresh Lake Erie Walleye filet into 2" pieces
1 lb perch filets, each cut in thirds
salt and cayenne pepper, to taste
a splash of Paramount Anisette, to taste
a mixture of snipped Italian parsley and fresh basil
sauce Rouille (recipe follows)

In a large, non-reactive kettle, lightly saute the onion in the olive oil. Add the fennel, leek, carrot, and garlic, stirring well to blend with the oil. Cover and braise over low heat for 10 minutes. Uncover and add the tomatoes, potato, thyme, bay leaf, saffron threads, and fish broth. Bring to the stove and simmer, partially covered, for 25 minutes. (Please note, the dish can be prepared ahead to this point and reheated just to the simmer at the time of completion.)

To continue, raise the heat and add the mussels. Cover and steam until the mussels open. Then add the shrimp, scallops, walleye, and perch. Cover and allow to sit over very low heat for an additional 5 minutes.

To serve, equally divide the shellfish and fish pieces between 8 large rimmed soup plates. Season the broth to taste with salt, cayenne pepper, and Paramount Anisette. Spoon the broth over the fish send the rest to table separately. Sprinkle each serving with snipped fresh parsley and fresh basil. Place a small dollop of sauce rouille in the center, passing the rest separately.

Sauce Rouille *(a piquant seasoning for bouillabaisse)*

1 clove of garlic, peeled
remainder of the green bell pepper, peeled, seeded, & diced
2 hot red peppers, CARE-

FULLY seeded and quartered (wear rubber gloves and dispose promptly)
1 tsp orange zest

2 tsp lemon zest
1/4 tsp salt
1 small cooked potato
hot fish broth

In a blender jar or in the workbowl of a food processor, combine the garlic, green pepper, hot peppers, orange and lemon zests, and salt. Process until well chopped and blended. Add the cooked potato and just enough hot fish broth to moisten the rouille to spoon consistency. Carefully check seasoning, adding additional salt and/or cayenne pepper as needed.

(This recipe was submitted by Tom Johnson, Corporate Chef, Paramount Distillers, Inc.)

Regional Suggestions

Restaurants:

Crescent Tavern
198 Delaware Ave
Put-in-Bay, OH 43456
(419) 285-4211

Kelley's Island Wine Company
418 Woodford Road
Kelleys Island, OH 43438
(419) 746-2678

Island Café & Brew Pub
504 Lakeshore Drive
Kelleys Island, OH 43438
(419) 746-2314
(800) 272-3815

Mon Ami Restaurant
3845 East Wine Cellar Road
Port Clinton, OH 43452
(440) 797-4445

Accommodations:

Bay House Bed & Breakfast
1360 Catawba Ave
Put-in-Bay, OH 43456
(419) 285-2822

Wisteria Inn Bed & Breakfast
1331 Langram Rd
Put-in-Bay, OH 43456
(419) 285-2828

The Eagle's Nest
216 Cameron Rd
Kelleys Island, OH 43438
(419) 746-2708

Zettler's Lakefront B&B
207 W. Lakeshore Drive
Kelleys Island, OH 43438
(419) 746-2315

Marblehead Inn
614 East Main St.
Marblehead, OH 43440
(419) 798-8184
(877) H_2O-View (426-8439)

Transportation to Islands:

Jet Express/Express Shuttle
Jet Express service to Put-in-Bay from Port Clinton, and Express
Shuttle from Put-in-Bay to Kelleys Island.
(800) 245-1538 • www.jet-express.com

Kelleys Island Ferry Boat Lines
Service from Marblehead to Kelleys Island.
(888) 225-4325

Miller Boat Line
Service from Catawba to Put-in-Bay and Middle Bass Island.
(800) 500-2421 • www.millerferry.com

Neuman Ferry Line
Service between Marblehead and Kellys Island.
(419) 626-5557 • (800) 876-1907 • www.neumanferry.com

Sonny-S Ferry
Service to Lonz Winery, Middle Bass, from Put-in-Bay.
(419) 285-8774

Local Attractions:

Alaskan Birdhouse Wildlife Museum
Meechen Rd • Put-in-Bay, OH 43456 • (419) 285-9736

Cedar Point Amusement Park
1 Causeway Dr • Sandusky, OH 44870 • (419) 626-0830

COSI Toledo (interactive science museum)
1 Discovery Way • Toledo, OH 43604-1579 • (419) 244-COSI

Northern Region

Good Company, Good Wine,
Good Welcome, Make Good People.

— Shakespeare

Lake Erie's Northern Region

Ontario is very large. The drive from Detroit, its southwestern gateway from the United States, to Buffalo, the southeasternmost gateway, is long, and at times, desolate. Beautifully desolate.

After driving through cluttered roadways, the roads through the counties bordering Lake Erie are a relief for any driver. The towns are quaint, but very lively, and everyone you'll encounter is exceptionally welcoming.

While Ontario has many, many more wineries than are included in this book, I wanted to focus on the few that are directly influenced by Lake Erie.

These wineries are situated on what is called the Lake Erie North

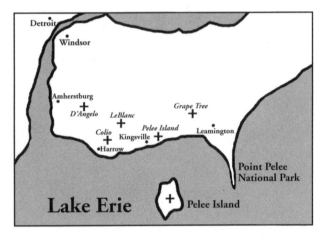

Shore Wine Route. Beginning just fifteen minutes southeast of Detroit, Michigan, the wine route winds through the scenic towns of Windsor, Amherstburg, Harrow, Kingsville and Leamington.

This route is expanding, with four wineries scheduled to open through 2002. As many of the current winemakers have said, the more the merrier. At this point, the region is often overlooked in favor of Canada's, and even Ontario's other wine regions.

Two of the largest wineries in the Lake Erie region sit proudly in Ontario. Colio Estate Winery and Pelee Island Winery, each producing over 200,000 cases a year, have helped put this region on the map. D'Angelo is about to change locations, moving the winery to a new site right on the shore. Soon, they'll be adding a restaurant and an inn. LeBlanc winery is doing things a little differently from the other North Shore wineries, creating traditional *vinifera* red wines – without the oak.

When traveling between the United States and Canada, please respect each country's customs limits. Feel free to buy all the wine you like, but be ready to pay import taxes when and where they are applicable.

Focus on the North Shore's Newest Star

Steven Brook, with the help of his wife and partners, is in the final planning stages of opening one of the North Shore's newest wineries, Grape Tree Estate Wines. The winery, which will be located in the tall-chimneyed building amidst the vineyards, should produce about 2,000 cases the first year.

"We're having great luck with Pinot," says Steven, who has grown grapes since 1994. Expect to see a couple different red wines offered when the winery opens its doors.

Grape Tree Estste Wines will be the eastern end of the North Shore Wine Route, and the only winery in Leamington, giving it a great advantage when it opens.

Drive by the winery and check for signs or ask the other North Shore wineries to find out when Grape Tree is officially open for business. Best of luck to Steven, his family and partners as they enter the North Shore wine industry.

Grape Tree's towering chimney marks the spot.

Grape Tree Estate Wines
308 Mersea Road 3
Leamington, ON N8H 3V5

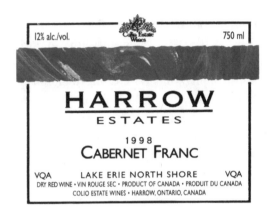

COLIO ESTATE WINES

Founded:	1980
Owners:	Enzo DeLuca & Joe Berardo
Winemaker:	Carlo Negri
Address:	1 Colio Drive
	Harrow, Ontario N0R 1G0
Phone:	(519) 738-2241, (800) 265-1322
WWW/E-mail:	www.colio.com, colio@total.net
Hours:	Monday - Friday 9 a.m. to 6 p.m.
	Saturday 10 a.m. to 6 p.m.
	Sunday 12 p.m. to 5 p.m.
Annual production:	200,000 cases
Price range of wines:	$3.25 - $18.95 ($41.95 for Ice Wine) CA
Amenities available:	Wheelchair accessible, restrooms.

Directions:

From Windsor, take Highway 18 south/east to Walker Road in Harrow. Turn left and follow to signs for the winery on your right.

From points east, take Highway 18 west to Walker Road, just east of Harrow. Go north and watch for the winery on your right.

From the road, Colio Estate Wines looks to be a large, non-descript warehouse. Once in the retail shop, you quickly learn that Colio creates a wide range of quality VQA wines suiting even the most discriminating palates.

The retail boutique, which includes a tasting bar, is fresh and finely decorated with artful displays of grapes and wine. Here you can sample any of Colio's twenty-some wines.

Colio offers wines under a few different brands, each one indicative of a unique style of winemaking. Colio Estate Vineyards (C.E.V.) and Harrow Estate wines are premium lines offering *vinifera* varietals including Cabernet Franc, Cabernet Sauvignon, Merlot, Sauvignon Blanc and Riesling, among others.

A tour of Colio's winery will reveal both modern facilities and hands-on artful winemaking processes.

Winemaker Carlo Negri has more than just juice, grapes and wine on his mind.

"We emphasize quality and affordable prices," says Negri, who believes the public should not be expected to pay a lot of money for exceptional wines.

Negri started making wine in 1963 in his native Italy. It was in 1980 that Colio asked him to lead its winery into the next century. He's been expanding the winery's operation ever since.

"We've more than doubled since our inception," says Negri,

insisting that the winery will continue growing in the coming years to keep up with intense regional demand for its wine.

Colio Estate Winery grows 50 percent of its grapes and buys the rest from regional growers. Their 180 acres of vines are wonderful, says Negri, but they cannot produce as many grapes as are needed.

Colio is not just expanding its traditional wine lines. The winery offers its own port and sherry and has plans for grappa and brandy. Expect to see even more wine on the shelves in the near future.

A tour of the winery shows just how large an operation Colio really is. The production room is cavernous and includes a fully-automated bottling and packaging line. The cellar includes a huge stainless steel tank room and an immaculate new barrel room.

Art, not just practicality, was applied to the plans of the new barrel room. Its sage colored floor and muraled walls give way to an altar of a private tasting area at the far end of the room. Over 300 American oak barrels are stacked in threes and lined in long rows, making this room as visually pleasing as it is useful.

*U*niquities:

- *Gorgeous new oak-aging facility with beautiful murals and floor.*
- *Many different lines of wines – all unique styles.*

"Come and unwined," says a sign on the road, luring travelers to the winery for a relaxing and informative experience. After an educating tour and a taste of Colio's wealth of wines, you too will have unwound and enjoyed your visit.

Wine Selections:

Cabernet Franc Reserve: Very smooth, few tannins and cherries.
Harrow Estate Merlot: Very nice, medium-bodied dry red.
Lily: Crisp sparkling white with fine bubbles and a great finish.

Maple Syrup & Orange Glazed Pork Tenderloin on Crispy Risotto Cake

Ingredients: Makes 12 pieces
12 ozs of leftover risotto
12 ozs of pork tenderloin
     (silver skin and fat removed)
4 oz maple syrup
1 orange, sliced
1 cinnamon stick (break into small pieces)
1 roasted red pepper – skin removed, cut 1/4" x 1/4" x 2"
1 roasted green pepper – skin removed, cut 1/4" x 1/4" x 2"
1 bunch thyme
4 oz olive oil

Risotto Cakes:

Form 1 oz of risotto into a small patty 1/2" thick.
Heat non-stick pan with 1 tablespoon of olive oil.
Fry cake until crispy on the outside.

Pork:

Slice pork into 1/2" thick medallions
Marinate with maple syrup, orange, 3 sprigs of thyme, cinnamon and olive oil. Grill pork until medium rare.

Place pork on top of risotto cake. Layer with a strip of each roasted pepper. Serve hot.

Serve with Harrow Estates Cabernet Franc.

(This recipe was submitted by Bill Grimshaw, Executive Chef of Sonoma County Wine Bar/Grille, Burlington, Ontario.)

D'ANGELO
ESTATE WINERY

Founded:	1983
Owner:	Sal D'Angelo and Partners
Winemaker:	Sal D'Angelo
Address:	5141 Concession 5, R.R. 4
	Amherstburg, Ontario N9V 2Y9
Phone:	(519) 736-7959
Hours:	Monday - Saturday 10 a.m. to 6 p.m.
	Sunday 11 a.m. to 5 p.m.
Annual Production:	12,000 cases
Price range:	$8.00 - $20.00 (Ice Wine, $46.50) CA

Directions:

From Windsor, take Highway 18 south. Turn left on County Road 10. Follow to Concession 5 and turn right. The winery will be on your left.

From points east, take Highway 18 west and up through Amherstburg. Turn right on County Road 10 and then right on Concession 5. The winery will be on your left.

"Local winery owner has ascended into royalty," reads a front-page article in an Essex County, Ontario, newspaper. Sal D'Angelo has been crowned a Grape King.

This most revered title among Ontario grape-growers has never, since its inception in 1946, been awarded to a grape-grower from the North Shore region.

The trophy reflects Sal's smile as he talks of D'Angelo Estate Winery's other prestigious awards. His ice wine has been awarded best in Ontario two years in a row. Sal's not stopping there, though.

"We're dedicating the next ten years to *vinifera*," says D'Angelo. He's excited about the growth of more great *vinifera* in the region.

D'Angelo is a fine winemaker, but it's his sense of humor and ease of conversation that make him who he is.

"We have three things to concentrate on: Quality, quality and

D'Angelo's ice wine grapes (seen covered by netting on right) must survive early winter, and hungry birds.

quality," he says in his most serious tone. He then laughs off the seriousness without diminishing his statement.

D'Angelo Winery's slogan is, "We make wine the natural way. We grow it." Sal believes that wine is made in the vineyard, and that if all is well on the vine, all will be well with the wine. Standing behind this belief, he has chosen a new vineyard site which will be the most southerly mainland vineyard in Canada. Moderated by the lake, this site should produce some of the finest grapes the North

Shore has ever seen.

D'Angelo is a former college professor with research still on his mind. He's been testing different trellis systems on his 40-acre vineyard for seventeen years to find out which works best in this region. He's also experimenting with Sangiovese and Syrah, two varieties that are uncommon on Lake Erie's North Shore.

Sal D'Angelo will soon move his winery to a new location located on the lake right next to his new vineyard site. Joining the winery will be a restaurant and an accompanying inn.

Uniquities:

- *Home of the North Shore's only "Grape King."*
- *Award-winning Vidal Ice Wine with intricate wood-cut label.*

"It's all part of our aggressive expansion program," says Sal. He's already planted ten acres of vines, with sixteen more ready for planting as soon as Sal has some time on his hands.

One of D'Angelo's new partners is Gus Moscatello. He is relatively new to wine but has found a new passion in D'Angelo's wine.

"It's like I've been watching black and white TV all my life -- now I'm looking at color," says Gus, referring to the revelations he's found in wine.

Make sure you meet Sal and get to know his enthusiasm about the region's winegrowing potential. You will surely find this same passion and enthusiasm in D'Angelo's wine.

Wine Selections:

Chardonnay/Pinot Blanc: Pleasant blend, crisp fruit, nice balance.
Cabernet Franc Rose: Very fruity, low tannins. Refreshing change.
Select Late Harvest Riesling: Very sweet – not *too* sweet – and lovely.

Recipe

Pasta del Grape King

Ingredients:
1 cup white dry wine (vidal from D'Angelo Estate Winery)
2 links Italian sausages, skinned and pulled apart
1 lb penne pasta (good quality)
2 large garlic cloves (chopped)
4-6 tbsp virgin olive oil
2 cups diced fresh plum tomatoes
3-5 medium portabella mushrooms
1 small Spanish onion sliced
1 large carrot sliced
2 cups of zucchini or broccoli or asparagus

In a large pot boil water with 1 tbsp of salt.

In a large skillet brown sausages and garlic in oil, (5-8 minutes), add the wine and reduce to medium heat.

At the same time add penne to boiling water and add the rest of the ingredients to sausage mixture. Cover skillet and cook for 5 minutes, uncover and simmer on low until pasta is cooked.

Drain pasta and mix with sausage. Serves 4. Boun apetito!

Serve with D'Angelo Cabernet Franc Rose.

(This recipe was submitted by Sal D'Angelo of D'Angelo Estate Winery.)

LeBLANC
ESTATE WINERY

Founded:	1983
Owners:	Lyse and Pierre LeBlanc
Winemaker:	Lyse LeBlanc
Address:	4716 Concession 4, R.R. 2
	Harrow, Ontario N0R 1G0
Phone:	(519) 738-9228
Hours:	Monday - Saturday 11 a.m. to 6 p.m.
	Sunday, 12 p.m. to 5 p.m.
WWW/E-mail:	leblanc@msni.net
Annual production:	2,200 cases
Price range:	$6.50 - $22.00 ($39.95 for Ice Wine) CA
Amenities available:	Wheelchair accessible, picnic tables.

Directions:

From Windsor, take Highway 18 south/east to County Rd 11. Turn left and follow to Concession 4. Turn right and watch for the winery on your left.

From points east, take Highway 18 west to County Road 11. Turn right and follow to Concession 4. Turn right and look for the winery on your left.

LeBlanc Estate Winery started when Lyse and Pierre LeBlanc planted some vines on their property. They planned only to sell the grapes and juice and had no intention of becoming a winery.

After making some wine for themselves, friends began prodding them to make the jump. "It sort of grew on us," claims winemaker and general manager Lyse LeBlanc.

"It seemed to be a natural progression," Lyse says. While it took great effort to finally open the facilities to the public, Lyse says her biggest challenge was learning how to fairly price her wines. With that hurdle long overcome, Lyse has been welcoming customers into her winery since being licensed in the early 1990s.

She still sells juice to local home winemakers, who all rave about

Eccentricities and excellent wines abound inside LeBlanc Estate Winery.

the quality of her grapes. "It's ready to drink right now," says one home winemaker who has only aged his juice for one month. "I'll let it age, but it's so good it's ready now!" he says bubbling with enthusiasm.

"I just do what I want," says Lyse, who has tried some non-traditional winemaking techniques. Lyse has boldly chosen not to oak some of her red wines. In a world of winemaking where most reds are over-oaked, Lyse has, in some cases, avoided oak altogether.

"I enjoy doing different styles of wines," Lyse says. LeBlanc's wines are each very different. The Chardonnay is oaky with high acid, which should make it a nice ager. The Pinot Blanc is delicate, while the Pinot Noir is pleasantly round with just enough oak aging to keep it smooth.

"Pinot Noir is the heartbreak grape," says Lyse, addressing its fickleness on the vine. Hers is very good, when oaked and even when the wine has not touched a barrel.

When you walk in the winery tasting room, you'll see the whole operation: the office, the lab, the oak barrels, and a tasting bar and a great fireplace. The walls are lively with colorfully painted angles that give it a fresh, artistic feel.

"Our goal is to not grow much bigger," says Lyse, who never wants to become a mass produc-

Uniquities:

- *Offers some unusually non-oaked red wines like Pinot Noir.*
- *Only female winemaker in the Lake Erie region.*

er. As it is now, LeBlanc Estate Winery is a family operation. The LeBlanc's children are all involved, and Lyse's mind is perpetually on the winery.

"Pierre gave me a pump for Christmas," says Lyse, smiling as she points to a new silver must pump. Her expressions prove her passion for this business.

"I love my life right now," Lyse says. You can taste it in every glass of her wines.

Wine Selections:

Pinot Noir (oaked): Soft and round with light oak and strawberries on the nose, cherries in the mouth.

Cabernet Sauvignon: Slight tannins and nice fruit in a hand-written labeled bottle.

Lyse's Grilled Shrimp

Ingredients:
2 lbs shelled jumbo shrimp
2 cloves garlic
2 tbsp oregano
2 tbsp parsley
1/2 tsp hot pepper flakes
1 cups bread crumbs
1/2 cups olive oil
salt and pepper to taste

In a large bowl mix all ingredients except shrimp, adding enough oil to bind ingredients into a light paste. Add shrimp. For best reults, mix with hands making sure some of the breadcrumbs stick to the shrimp. Skewer the shrimp and grill until opaque. Best served hot, but delicious at room temperature.

Serve with LeBlanc Dry Riesling.

(This recipe was submitted by Lyse LeBlanc of LeBlanc Estate Winery.)

PELEE ISLAND
WINERY

Founded:	1982
Owners:	Privately Owned
Winemakers:	Walter Schmoranz and Martin Janz
Address:	455 Seacliff Drive
	Kingsville, Ontario, Canada N9Y 2K5
Phone:	(519) 733-6551, (800) 59-PELEE
WWW/E-mail:	www.peleeisland.com, pelee@mnsi.net
Hours:	Winery open year-round
	Monday - Saturday 9 a.m. to 6 p.m.,
	Sun 11 a.m. to 5 p.m.
	Pavilion open from May to October
Annual production:	250,000 cases
Price range of wines:	$7.95 - $24.95 ($39.95 for Ice Wine) CA
Amenities available:	Restrooms, ferry which leaves from winery.

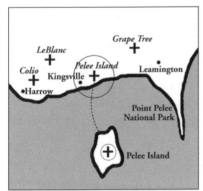

Directions:

From Windsor, take Highway 18 south/east to Kingsville. The winery is on the right. Ferries to the Pelee Island Wine Pavilion leave

From points east, take Highway 3 to Kingsville and look for the winery on the left.

Imagine an island of grapes, sitting just south of the rest of its country, in the middle of a huge, climate-moderating lake. Now imagine the winery that makes the fine wine from the island's 500 acres of vines.

Welcome to Pelee Island Winery.

Depending on where you're coming from, you'll either visit the mainland winery and home base of the winery, or the Wine Pavilion located on the island itself. To get a complete feel for the many facets of Pelee Island Winery, you must visit both, as they each are great adventures.

The mainland winery is the production house. Each year during harvest, a ferry brings the grapes from the island vineyards to the mainland winery's docks (leaving some room for tourists, too!). With its cellar of large oak barrels and huge stainless steel tanks, the winery is immense.

The retail shops at both locations offer tours of the facilities as

Rows of vines meet the Lake at Pelee Island's Wine Pavilion.

well as demonstration videos on how Pelee's wine is made. The mainland shop has a great tour of the full winery, including a tasting of five wines. The tasting room, located below the retail shop, is filled with long wooden tables complemented with two large, private wine-barrel booths.

One of the first things you'll notice is the friendly label design on each of Pelee's wines. Many have been inspired by local lore or by indigenous wildlife and would make colorful additions to your wine collection.

Before it reaches the bottle, though, Wine Master Walter Schmoranz takes great care to ensure the quality of every wine. The wine list includes over 30 wines, including their prized ice wine, their many VQA *vinifera* wines, and "house" wines and blends. All their wines are available at both locations, and are made from grapes grown on Pelee Island.

If you have the opportunity to visit the island's Wine Pavilion, allow time for the ferry rides there and back, and some leisure activities once you get there – like appreciating the unique flora and fauna of Pelee Island.

Visiting the island from either side of the lake is easy. From Ontario, catch the Pelee Island Ferry from Leamington (March to August) or Kingsville (August to December). From Ohio, catch one of the ferries from Sandusky or Port Clinton. One of Pelee Island Winery's travel trams will pick you up and guide you to the pavilion, saving you from bringing your car or renting transportation on the island.

The Wine Pavilion is spacious and offers many outside activities and picnic areas. Concerts and other events fill the summer calendar making it a good possibility you'll stumble into a party when you visit. But no matter which of Pelee's sites you visit, be prepared for a multitude of wonderful wine.

Uniquities:

- *Separate "Wine Pavilion" on Pelee Island (with direct access by ferry from the winery).*
- *Great assortment of wines.*

Wine Selections:

Gamay Noir Zweigelt, VQA: Light, fruity red with a hint of spice.
Gewürtzraminer, VQA: Semi-sweet and lively with peaches and mangos on the nose, and floral, herb and spice flavors.

Late Harvest Riesling with Catalan-Style Chicken in a Velvety Wine Sauce

Ingredients:
4 boneless, skinless chicken breasts
1/2 cup flour
pinch of salt
pinch of pepper
2 tbsp olive oil
1 onion, chopped
2 garlic cloves, chopped
2/3 cup blanched almonds
1/2 tsp cinnamon
pinch of nutmeg
1/2 *(generous)* cup Pelee Island Late Harvest Riesling
1/2 cup water
pinch of saffron
4 egg yolks

Sprinkle the chicken with flour, salt and pepper on both sides. Heat the oil in a frying pan over high heat.

Add the chicken and cook until lightly browned, about 2 minutes on each side. Push the chicken to one side of the pan and add the onion, garlic, almonds and spices.

Cook for 3 minutes, add wine, water and saffron. Bring to a boil, reduce to half (this will take approximately 7-8 minutes).

Remove pan from heat and place the chicken breasts on a serving plate. Whisk the egg yolks in the sauce and stir until sauce is velvety.

Pour over chicken and serve immediately. Serves 4.

(This recipe was submitted by the staff of Pelee Island Winery.)

Regional Suggestions

Restaurants:

Duffy's Tavern & Motor Inn
306 Dalhousie Street
Amherstburg, ON N9V 1X3
(516)736-4301

The Gallery
11 Queens St.
Leamington, Ontario N8H 3G5
(519) 322-2399

Kings Landing
103 Park Street
Kingsville, Ontario
(519) 733 2336

Anchor & Wheel Inn
11 West Shore Rd.
Pelee Island, ON N0R 1M0
(519) 724-2195

Vintage Goose
24 W. Main St.
Kingsville, Ontario N9Y 1H1
(519) 733-6900

The Tin Goose Inn
1060 East West Rd.
Pelee Island, ON N0R 1M0
(519) 724-2223

Accommodations:

B&B's Bed and Breakfast
216 Erie St. S.
P.O. Box 98
Wheatley, ON N0P 7P0
(519) 825-8008

The Gathering Place
West Shore Road
Pelee Island, ON N0R 1M0
(519) 724-2656

Island Memories
192 North Shore Dr.
Pelee Island, ON N0R 1M0
(519) 724-2667

Drifters Inn
144 King St. W.
Harrow, Ontario
(519) 738-9303

Kingswood Inn
10 Mill St. West.
Kingsville, ON N9Y 1W4
(519) 733-3248

The Wedding House
98 Main St. E.
Kingsville, ON N9Y IA4
(519) 733-3928

Stonehill Bed & Breakfast
911 West Shore Road
Pelee Island, ON N0R 1M0
(519) 724-2193

The Patrician Inn
1399 Front Rd. N.
Amherstburg, Ontario
(519) 736 1549

Local Attractions:

Colasonti's Tropical Gardens
Ruthven, Ontario • N0P 2G0 • (519) 326-3287
www.colasanti.com

Fish Point & Lighthouse Point on Pelee Island

Jack Miner Bird Sanctuary
Kingsville, Ontario N9Y-2E8 • (519) 733-4034
www.jackminer.com

John R. Park Homestead & Conservation Area

Pelee Island Heritage Center

Willistead Manor, Windsor

Good Information

Deep roots in the land anchor life.

— *Paul Roberts*

Wine Festivals

Wine festivals provide a great opportunity for wine lovers to try may different wines without driving all over the region. For a fee, you get to try lots of wine while listening to music and eating great food! And, if you're interested in volunteering at one of the wineries' tents, let them know – they always need help!

Many of the wineries hold their own events, celebrating new wine releases or just about any excuse to invite people over for a good time. While there are no Lake Erie regional wine festivals, each of the states and Ontario hold events promoting their own local industry's wines. The major wine festivals are typically held on weekends throughout the summer.

The best way to find out about the festivals is by checking with the individual wineries. They will either have pamplets for the festivals or can tell you who to get in-touch with for more details.

Also, check the websites listed below for up-to-date event listings.

New York Wine & Grape Foundation
www.nywine.com

Ohio Wine Producers Association
www.ohiowine.org

Pennsylvania Wine Association
www.pennsylvaniawine.com

Wine Council of Ontario
www.wineroute.com

Regional Wine Associations

These associations are good resources for anyone interested in wine, grapes, and the industry as a whole.

American Institute of Wine and Food
1-800-274-AIWF, National Office
call for local chapters

American Wine Society
(716) 225-7613 • aws@vicon.net
contact for local chapters

Lake Erie Quality Wine Association
(800) 600-WINE • www.lakeeriewine.com

New York Wine & Grape Foundation
350 Elm Street • Penn Yan, NY 14527
315-536-7442; FAX 315-536-0719
www.nywine.com

Ohio Wine Producers Association
(440) 466-4417 • (800) 227-6972 • www.ohiowines.org

Ontario Vintners Quality Alliance
110 Hannover Drive • Suite B205 • St. Catharines, ON L2W 1A4
(905) 684-8070, (905) 684-2993 fax

Pennsylvania Wine Association
(877) 4-PA-WINE • www.pennsylvaniawine.com

Wine Publications

Magazines:
Wine Enthusiast 1-800-356-8466
Wine Spectator 1-800-395-3364
> Both of these magazines offer reviews of wines and informative articles and columns about wine, wine regions around the world, and general wine appreciation.

Books:
The University Wine Course. Marion W. Baldy.
San Francisco: Wine Appreciation Guild, 1997.
> This is a college text, but it provides wonderful information in a very smart format for anyone interested in furthering their knowledge of wines and winemaking.

Wineries of the Great Lakes, A Guidebook. Joe Borrello.
Lapeer, MI: Raptor Press, 1995.
> Great quick-guide to all the wineries in the Great Lakes wine regions. The book's one page per winery gives basic details and insights. Worth keeping in the glove compartment for road-trips!

How To Be A Wine Expert. James Gabler.
Baltimore, MD: Bacchus Press, 1995
> Gabler takes great care to decode the mystery behind wine. Once read, you'll be much more knowledgable about many wine topics.

Wine for Dummies. Ed McCarthy. Mary Ewing-Mulligan.
Foster City, CA: IDG Books International, 1995.
> You can't go wrong with this book if you want an introduction to wine. It's written very simply and is a great help for beginning wine drinkers.

Where to Buy Lake Erie Wines

This is a difficult region to deal with when it comes to finding the wines you want *outside* the wineries' retail stores. In Pennsylvania and Ontario, there are Liquor Control Board stores that tend to sell only certain local wines (although they can order *any* wine if you ask nicely). In New York and Ohio, you have a better chance of finding the wines you're looking for.

Having wine shipped to your home directly from wineries is yet another difficulty. Each state/province has different laws on who can ship and who can receive. Of those covered in this book, none allow wine to be shipped into their state from another state. These laws are always on the move, so check the law before you attempt to ship anything yourself.

Here are the best ways to find your favorite Lake Erie wines:
1. The easiest way to get your favorite regional wines is to purchase directly from the winery. If you find something you like, buy it by the case at the winery because most will give a 10-20 percent discount on all case purchases.

2. Buy from the wineries at one of the annual festivals. This is a great opportunity to try many wines and buy as much as you like in one trip.

3. Buy from your local wine merchant or Liquor Control Board store. Most Lake Erie regional wines are distributed throughout the immediate area, especially from the larger wineries. When you visit a winery, ask if and where their wines are available in your area.

Useful Wine Terms

ACIDITY - the essential natural element that gives wine its crispness on the palate. Too much and the wine will seem hard or bitter. Too little and the wine will seem flabby. Good acid levels help a wine age well.

AFTERTASTE - the taste left in the mouth (good or bad) after the wine has been swallowed.

APPELLATION - a grape growing area designated and governed by the federal government.

AROMA - the fragrance of the grape. What the winemaker does and the wine-making techniques used evolve into nuances of smell that are called "bouquet."

BALANCE - the harmony of all a wine's components – sugar, fruit, tannin, wood, and alcohol. Wines where one or more component stands out and dominates the wine are considered out of balance.

BODY - a wine may be deemed full-bodied, medium-bodied or medium-weight, or light-bodied after an assessment of its weight on the palate. Alcohol, glycerin and sugar all play into a wine's texture and weight.

COMPLEX - one of the most subjective descriptive terms used, a complex wine should have lots of different smells and flavors that seem to change with each sip.

DEPTH - wine with depth has a concentration of flavors, a rich intensity, and tends to be mouth-filling.

DRY - the opposite of sweet. A wine is dry when all of the sugar in the grapes has been fermented into alcohol. The acid content may also determine the sense of dryness.

FINISH - the aftertaste, also called length. All wine has a finish, whether it is short or long, pleasant or unpleasant. A long and/or pleasant finish is preferable to a short and/or unpleasant finish.

FIRST-RUN/FREE-RUN JUICE - when grapes are placed in a press, those that are the ripest will burst on their own. This juice is called "free-run" because it has not actually been pressed from the grapes. Since it is the ripest, most intense juice of the crop, it is typically used as a wine of its own, or blended to improve the rest of the juice once pressed.

FOXY - term often used to describe the earthy, musky character of wines made from North American *labrusca* grapes.

FRUITY - conveying an impression of fruit, sometimes grapes, but often other kinds of fruit, including raspberries, peaches, apricots, cherries, black currants, etc. A fruity wine can be completely dry, with no residual sugar.

FULL-BODIED - wines rich in grape extract, alcohol, and glycerine are full-bodied.

HYBRID - a cross between a hardier native American grape (*labrusca*) variety and one of European descent.

JAMMY - a term describing intensely ripe, rich fruit flavors and aromas in a wine

LABRUSCA (*vitis labrusca*) - the main North American vine species; extremely resistant to extreme weather conditions and to frost. Examples are Concord and Catawba.

LEGS - after swirling a wine in a glass, it creeps back down the sides of the glass and back into the bowl. Generally, slower the streaks (legs) are to fall back down, the more full-bodied the wine is. Legs are sometimes called tears, too.

SMOKY - another self-explanatory term, describing the flavor of some barrel-aged wines. Can also be a result of certain soil types.

SMOOTH - self-explanatory term, used to describe the texture and finish of a wine.

SOFT - describes a wine lacking the bite of tannins or acids

SULFITES - when a label reads "Contains Sulfites," it means sulfur dioxide was used in the process of grape growing or winemaking. Persons allergic to sulfites should be cautious when choosing their wines.

SWEET - one of the four basic tastes perceived by the tongue, as opposed to the hundreds of flavors that we actually experience with our olfactory senses. The presence of sugar (or occasionally of glycerine) is required to taste sweetness.

TANNIN - one of the key acids found in wine. It comes from the skins, seeds, and stems of the grapes. This is what makes your mouth pucker when drinking a red wine, especially a young one. Tannin is what gives wine its longevity and dryness.

VARIETAL - a wine made from at least 75 percent of one grape variety.

VINIFERA (*Vitis Vinifera*) - 99 percent of all wines are made from this grape species. There are thousands of varieties of this species, most notably Chardonnay, Cabernet Sauvignon, Merlot, Pinot Noir, Riesling, and Zinfandel.

VINTAGE - the year of a harvest and when the wine was made.

Discover Other Titles from

resonant ◉ publishing

Discovering Lake Erie Wineries
by Kevin Atticks
ISBN: 0-9668716-3-4
$11.95

Discovering Maryland Wineries
by Kevin Atticks
ISBN: 0-9668716-0-X
$9.95

From this hill, my hand, Cynthiana's Wine
by Paul Roberts
ISBN: 0-9668716-2-6
$16.95/each

Discovering . . . Wineries
by Kevin Atticks
Many more titles of this popular series
are planned. Check out website for
the latest offerings.

Thanks for your interest, and we hope you enjoy all of our publications.
For more information, please visit us online at:
www.resonantgroup.com

Send all inquiries to:

resonant ◉ publishing

info@resonantgroup.com • www.resonantgroup.com
(603) 462-5675 *fax*

Notes

Notes

—— *Notes* ——

— *Notes* —

Notes

Notes